Oswego County and the Civil War

OSWEGO COUNTY AND THE CIVIL WAR

They Answered the Call

NATALIE JOY WOODALL

THE History PRESS

Published by The History Press
Charleston, SC 29403
www.historypress.net

Opposite: This pillar honors soldiers from New Haven who died in the Civil War. Among them was Granville Woodall. *Author's collection.*

First published 2013

Manufactured in the United States

ISBN 978.1.62619.208.9

Library of Congress CIP data applied for.

This book is dedicated to all Oswego County men who served the Union cause, especially my great-great-grandfather John Joseph Woodall and his brother, Granville Sharp Woodall.

"All gave some—some gave all."

Contents

Preface

And we are but poor players.

Inspiration for this book was kindled when I became interested in the Lord and the Adriance families, who lived in Oswego City and Scriba Town in the mid-nineteenth century. I discovered that three Lord daughters had married Civil War veterans, one of whom was an Adriance. A fourth married the brother of a veteran.

The girls' father, Reverend Alfred Chapman Lord (1805–1896), was a descendant of Solomon Lord of Connecticut. His grandson, Zelotes Lord (1771–1850), and wife, Sarah Farnham (1774–1859), moved from Connecticut to Oneida County, New York, where their son Alfred was born in Rome. He married Laura Partridge Blossom (1817–1888) in 1836. They probably migrated to Oswego County sometime prior to daughter Sarah's birth in 1837 since both the 1855 and the 1865 census records state that all their children were born there.

Alfred and Laura produced eleven offspring. Except for Ida Arletta (1855–1857) and Jane Eliza (1861–1863), all grew to adulthood. The men whose lives are explored in this book were married to Lydia (1839–1927), Abbie (1844–1926) and Catherine (1851–1904). Sarah (1837–1915) was married to Joshua, a brother of Otis, one of this book's subjects. Although not directly involved in this story, Sarah was probably the sibling to whom the others turned in times of trouble.

The goal of this book was not to chronicle my subjects' military careers, which in two cases were brief, but rather to explore their circumstances after

The Lord family monument is located in the North Scriba Cemetery. *Author's collection.*

This detail of the Lord family monument commemorates Reverend Alfred C. Lord and his wife of many years, Laura P. Blossom. *Author's collection.*

their army days ended. I have described certain military events, but my intention has been to tell "the rest of the story"; that is, what happened when these men returned home. War does terrible things to men, and the Lord sisters were exemplars of the misery wives endured while caring for husbands left incapacitated by war service.

I have attempted to include as much family history as possible. These men had parents, siblings, children and in-laws who influenced their lives. Sometimes, I have been able to correct other researchers' findings because of my proximity to cemeteries, the Oswego County Record Office and the Oswego Public Library. If, however, I have included erroneous information, I take full responsibility.

Nineteenth-century spelling was not as regular as it is today. Many people could not spell their own names, depending on others to do it for them or witnessing their "X." Census records are not always trustworthy. For example, Himan Dutcher said in one census that he did not know where his parents were born. In others, he correctly stated that his father was born in New York State and his mother in Canada. People frequently lied to the enumerators about birthplace and age. Even tombstones contain inaccuracies. A good example is that of Lydia Lord Adriance. Although the family stone in Riverside Cemetery in Scriba states that she died in 1928, her death actually occurred in 1927, as evidenced by her obituary.

Military records provide a wealth of information. Personal characteristics such as hair and eye color and height will be found.

Depositions for pension applications are interesting. Francis Pease spent time in three Confederate prisons and suffered the effects of his confinement for the rest of his short life.

William Adriance, Francis Pease, Otis Miner, Frederick Marvin and Himan Dutcher represent a sampling of the thousands of Oswego County Civil War veterans whose stories await investigation. Names of those mentioned in this text may provide impetus for further research. For example, Gilbert Dutcher and William Henry Horton, whose stories cannot be included here because of space constraints, deserve investigation. Perhaps the content of this book will encourage others to undertake similar research.

Natalie Joy Woodall
Oswego, New York

Acknowledgements

Much of this book is based on primary sources, and I thank the National Archives for helping me obtain military and pension files. I also thank the Oswego Public Library for its wonderful collection of cemetery records, historical newspapers and books. Justin White, Oswego County Historian, was always willing to answer questions and look up information. Paul Lear, site manager of Fort Ontario, generously provided information on Joshua Hibbard. No one can write local history without the assistance of Tom Tryniski's wonderful website, www.fultonhistory.com. I tender genuine gratitude to The History Press for having sufficient confidence in my book to publish it. My commissioning editor, Whitney Landis, and project editor, Will Collicott, both deserve a tip of the hat for their patience and guidance.

I thank the Drake Oil Museum for permission to publish the photo of the oil fields at Shamburg, Pennsylvania; Charles Young and the Scriba Historical Society for permission to publish a photo of Himan Dutcher in his uniform; University of Virginia's Alderman Library for the autograph of Benson John Lossing's letter to Governor Morgan; Michael Hill of the North Carolina Office of Archives and History; Patricia Zwick, an Adriance descendant, for permission to use a photo of Charles Henry Evans; and Marian Stinson for information on Reverend Walter H. Moore.

I would be remiss if I did not mention my long-suffering friends Darlene Woolson and Lynda Seeley, who listened to the latest discoveries about "my men" and helped me scour cemeteries for graves and gravestones. To my "tekkie" friend Joanne Paino, I offer sincere gratitude for your computer skills. My wonderful stepmother, Keitha Woodall, supported me the many years I was engaged in this project. If I have omitted anybody's name, let me hasten to reassure one and all that I am most grateful for advice and knowledge.

Introduction

A Call to Arms

The issue of slavery plagued the colonies and, later, the fledgling states almost from the first time Europeans set foot on American soil, and while the center of the practice is generally thought to be in the South, slaves could be found as far north as Massachusetts. In 1776, approximately fifteen thousand slaves were living in New York State. Not until 1800 was the practice abolished in the northern states.

Unlike the northern states, which formed the industrial base of the country, the southern states were agricultural in nature, depending mostly on an economy of cotton and rice, necessitating large numbers of workers to prepare and harvest the crops. Additionally, the prevailing moral ethic was that slavery was good for slaves since they were being exposed to the "superior culture" of the white man. This belief was reinforced by ministers who preached that since Christ did not condemn slavery, he must have supported it.

As any American schoolchild knows, the problem of slavery vexed many of the Patriots who recognized the hypocrisy between the lofty sentiment "all men are created equal" and the reality that thousands of men, women and children were held in bondage. That the problem bothered the founding fathers is borne out by the way a compromise for taking a census of slaves appeared in the U.S. Constitution, according to which a slave represented three-fifths of a white person.

Opposition to slavery began early in the nation's history, starting with a protest by Quakers in Germantown, Pennsylvania, in 1688. Protests gained momentum and became organized in the early years of the nineteenth century. For example, William Lloyd Garrison founded the American Anti-Slavery Society in 1833. By 1837, New York State contained 274 abolitionist groups, and 45 of them were located in the North Country.

Oswego County residents were loud in their support of abolitionism. By 1856, antislavery proponents had grown to about four thousand. In the November 21, 1856 edition of the *Oswego Daily Times*, one writer noted, "Our county has done nobly. The principle of non-extension of slavery has taken deep root in the hearts of our free population. The voice of Oswego is in favor of making Kansas a free state."

As part of their commitment to the abolitionist movement, many Oswego County residents were participants in the Underground Railroad. Fleeing slaves made their way north to secret "stations," where they found temporary shelter, food and clothing. Mexico, New York, was an early center of abolitionism. In September 1835, seventy residents of that town signed a petition to Congress calling for the end of slavery in the District of Columbia. Mexico was also an important stop on the Underground Railroad.

Eleven sites in the city of Oswego and thirty-four throughout the county have been identified as stations on the Underground Railroad. Among the foremost of these in the city was the home of Edwin and Charlotte Clark. Edwin was one of Oswego's most outspoken abolitionists. The Clarks built a farmhouse and barn where they hid runaways who had succeeded in making their way to Oswego. It is estimated that Edwin and Charlotte helped about 125 fugitives reach safety. In 1842, Clark became president of the Oswego County Anti-Slavery Society. He wrote the following to the *Oswego Palladium*: "The principles of slavery and liberty are never dormant, never stand still. They are at constant war, each striving for its own life and conscious that it can exist only by the annihilation of the other." Of course, not everyone was an abolitionist. Many people opined that slavery was not unconstitutional and therefore was no one's business but the southerners'.[1]

Passage of the Fugitive Slave Act in 1850 further fueled opposition to slavery, as it permitted bounty hunters to capture and return runaways to their owners, no matter where they were taken. Slaves arrested in a free state had no legal recourse to being sent back to their masters. Bounties were placed on their heads, and the hunters also had a right to recoup expenses, giving added incentive to hunt them down.

It was inevitable that the churches become embroiled in the controversy. Reverend Mason Gallagher of Episcopal Church of the Evangelists caused

The Clark monument is dedicated to early Oswego abolitionists. *Author's collection.*

dissension among his congregation by delivering a series of antislavery sermons, speculating that he expected several families to transfer to Christ Church. He is quoted as saying, "I have given offense to all the so-called conservatives in town, but I believe there is virtue enough in the place to sustain the untrammeled and fearless preaching of the gospel. I will persevere with the help of God."[2] Gallagher exerted a great influence on the young men in his congregation. So great were his powers of persuasion that "[w]hile he was at Oswego, in response to a call for soldiers in 1861, he and seventy men in his congregation enlisted."[3] Gallagher served as chaplain for the Twenty-fourth Volunteer Regiment for almost a year.

Christ Church, the other Episcopal church in Oswego, joined the fray when its pastor, Reverend Anthony Schuyler, announced that slavery was not a "heinous sin" in 1861. His words caused more uproar in the church communities.[4]

The simmering debate between the northern and the southern states boiled over into violence on April 12, 1861, when Confederate forces fired on Fort Sumter in Charleston, South Carolina, forcing the small garrison to surrender. Three days later, President Abraham Lincoln issued the first call for troops, ordering a draft of 75,000 men to put down the insurrection. At the time, less than 1,000 men comprised the Regular Army east of the

The monument dedicated to all Oswego County soldiers contains this plaque. The statue stands in Franklin Park, Oswego. *Author's collection.*

Mississippi River. 350,000 men offered their services to the government, illustrating clearly the desire to quash "an uprising which was then generally considered as little more than a short-lived riot."[5] In Oswego County alone, between 11,000 and 12,000 men answered the call to arms. These estimates represent about 15 percent of the entire population and 75 percent of the voting population.[6] For example, the town of Scriba alone volunteered over 250 of its young men to the Union cause. By the time the war ended, Oswego County had provided ten complete infantry and cavalry regiments and parts of fourteen others. Additionally, many enlisted in the Regular Army.[7] Enthusiasm for the war was so high that underage boys enlisted.

For four long years, the citizenry of this country fought each other on bloody battlefields. When peace finally arrived in 1865, the South was a wasteland. Lincoln's plan for reconciliation was cut short with his assassination. Soldiers on both sides dragged themselves home and attempted to reintegrate into civilian life. For many, their time on earth would be short because of extensive wounds and ravaging disease. Those who managed to survive a longer period suffered incessantly from their experiences and eventually succumbed to their afflictions. Minuscule pensions doled out by the government did little to compensate for the pain and suffering of faithful and loyal soldiers and sailors. Johnny did not come marching home; rather, he was limping.

Chapter 1

William Henry Adriance

A man of good family and above the average in intelligence and education.

The *Ryerson Genealogy*, the standard compilation for the Adriance family, shows that William Henry Adriance was a direct descendant of Elbert (1663–?) and Catalyntie Remsen Vander Beeck Adriance (1655–1710). Elbert was a son of Adriens Reyersz, who immigrated to the New World in 1646 and settled in Flatbush, Long Island. His great-great-grandson Abraham J. Adriance (1773–1821) and Mary Elizabeth Eyrauld Van Vleeck (1778–ca.1842) were the parents of Henry Adriance (1805–1865), who became a bookbinder. He married Mary Eliza Beach (1810–1865) on September 29, 1831, at St. George's Church in New York City.

Henry and Mary's first child, William Henry, was born on August 5, 1832. The *Ryerson Genealogy* states that four more were born in New York. Alice was the first baby actually born in Oswego (1843), thereby establishing an approximate date for the family's migration to the area. The December 29, 1843 *Fulton Mirror* announced that Henry Adriance was "proprietor of [the] New York Store" in Fulton. It is possible that he had two stores, since a classified advertisement published in 1851 tends to confirm the former date. Referring to the refurnishing of his bookstore in Oswego, Adriance boasted, "Having been brought up in his business, he flatters himself he fully understands it, and by punctuality and attention, he hopes to merit a continuance and increase of that patronage so liberally extended to him for the past eight years."[8]

Henry Adriance believed in advertising liberally and sometimes placed as many as three classified ads in one paper. His stock ran the gamut from books, magazines and pens to newspapers and blank books. He also made use of the city directory to advertise his wares, as evidenced by the 1852 edition (page 104). We shall return to Henry's experiences later in the chapter.

A small announcement in an issue of a local newspaper revealed that William H. Adriance had purchased a paper and magazine business formerly owned by a "Mr. Spencre." Henry Adriance's 1859 directory advertisement included a small section at the bottom for the benefit of his son's business, located at No. 2 Jones Block. From this meager evidence, we may infer that Henry approved of his son's venture. It is well documented that Oswego was home to several book and magazine stands, all eagerly vying for the public's attention.

While one can only speculate, the reason for William's decision to leave the family bookstore and strike out on his own may have been his desire to marry. His first wife was Lois Loretta Strobeck. Because William was boarding at 31 West Oneida Street with his parents in 1857 but had his own home at 131 West Fifth Street in 1859, it is possible the couple was wed that year. Little is known about Lois. She appears only in the 1850 census for Verona, Oneida County, where she was living with Susan Strobeck, relationship unknown. Lois's name is misspelled as Louis, and her age is given as fourteen. How or why she moved to Oswego remains a mystery—nor do we have evidence for the way she and William met, although it is well documented that other Strobecks lived in Oswego.

William and Lois's marriage was short-lived. Her tombstone in the Adriance family plot in Riverside Cemetery states that she died on April 27, 1860, at the age of twenty-three years, eleven months and five days; she likely died in childbirth.

A little less than a year had passed after Lois's death when the Civil War erupted. Soon after the outbreak of hostilities, William H. Adriance volunteered for service in the Union army. He was twenty-eight and no doubt influenced by patriotic fervor among local civic and religious leaders. Adriance was a member of a company raised by Captain Edward Paine and was elected second sergeant by the group, perhaps because of his education and standing in the community.[9] The organization, under the general command of Colonel Timothy Sullivan, was designated the Twenty-fourth Infantry Regiment, one of several Oswego County was to provide for the war effort. The Twenty-fourth was also called the Oswego County Regiment because, of its eight companies, seven were recruited there. William was assigned to Company B, one of the four composed of men from the city of Oswego.

Enrollment took place swiftly, and Company A, under the command of Captain John D. O'Brien, left Oswego for Elmira on April 26. Adriance was elected second sergeant of Company B on April 29, and his group left Oswego by train, together with Captain Miller's Company C, on the morning of May 3, 1861. An enthusiastic crowd saw them off: "At the Railroad, there were at least ten thousand people assembled. As the cars moved off, three hearty cheers were given for the Oswego Volunteers, and three more for the American Union."[10]

Lois Strobeck Adriance was buried in the family plot. *Author's collection.*

A letter from "S," a volunteer in the Twenty-fourth, sent from Elmira and dated May 17, describes the condition at Camp Rathbun: "We are encamped in a building formerly used for a 'barrel factory.' The sheds and barns were cleaned and are now occupied by unfortunate volunteers. We sleep in the aforesaid barns in two-story bunks, built of the coarsest kind of hemlock. It is considered more dangerous to encounter the splinters of these bunks than to meet and receive a charge of bayonets. We sleep on straw mattrasses [*sic*] covered by a single blanket."[11] S's letter is important because in later life, Adriance steadfastly maintained he had acquired his affliction during the time he spent at Elmira.

Although Adriance never applied for a pension, his widow, Lydia, did under the provisions of several acts for the benefit of widows and orphans. To qualify, she was required to obtain depositions from persons who knew her husband while he was a member of the Twenty-fourth Regiment. Among these was George Stoffel. When questioned about the onset of Adriance's disability, Stoffel said it occurred "on or about the 25th day of May, 1861… by reason of exposure." Stoffel further stated that he had seen "the said Adriance whilst so sick, and going in company with him to a water cure in Elmira to be treated."[12] Another witness, Merrick Stowell, also a member of Company B and, later, an Oswego County judge, gave the following testimony: "That the said Adriance while in the line of his duty at Elmira in the State of New York on or about the last days of May 1861 contracted rheumatism and was absent from said company for the period of about three weeks for treatment for the same. That deponent knew this by reason of having been a member of said company at the time and recollecting that said Adriance was so absent and that he was reported to be sick with rheumatism."[13]

Two other deponents, Gale Kingsley and Edwin Huntington, recalled hearing Adriance complain of rheumatism at other times. Although Kingsley could not say with certainty that Adriance had complained at Elmira, he reported, "I think he was complaining at Bristol Sta., VA."[14] The regiment had been ordered to Bristol Station in the spring of 1862.[15] Huntington, a private in Company B, recalled, "Mr. Adriance was ailing a good deal while in the service. I remember he was complaining at Upton's Hill in particular and at other places and was absent from his command some on account of illness. My remembrance is his complaint was rheumatism."[16] The Twenty-fourth Regiment went to Upton's Hill in the fall of 1861, built Fort Upton and then spent the winter there.[17]

In addition to the primitive accommodations at Elmira, the food was also unfit for humans. S commented, "Would that I could obtain the aid of Wisdom's Goddess to supply opprobrious epithets to be used in connection with the food and contractors. We have literally 'nothing to eat and plenty of it.' Beef and potatoes of the cheapest kind, with once in a while pork and beans and very weak coffee comprise volunteer's fare. This is the dark side of our life."[18] William Henry Adriance, older than the typical recruit and a city dweller, was accustomed to sleeping in a warm, well-upholstered bed and eating a decent, varied diet. He worked in a bookstore, not on a farm, and his body was undoubtedly less tough than those of his comrades in arms. Therefore, it is easy to believe that he contracted a debilitating disease shortly after arriving in the camp.

A further blow was dealt to the regiment in June. S.H. Brown wrote, "Our men are having the measles in good earnest at this present time. We have about fifty cases on hand, and I think there will be enough to furnish all who have not had them."[19] This outbreak might have exacerbated Adriance's condition if he was already in a weakened state.

A related issue was the fact that uniforms and weaponry were non-existent. A letter from Captain Edward Paine, dated May 4, was published on May 7. In it, he encouraged Oswegonians to assist the men: "[Captain Paine] says blankets are greatly needed by the men. Some other things would not be amiss, such as towels, stockings and woolen shirts. Blankets and under clothes are wanted badly."[20] When H.C. Stearns announced plans to shuttle friends and relatives of the men to Elmira for a visit, the volunteers were reluctant to receive them. S.H. Brown, writing from the barracks on June 9, said, "We regret very much that the excursion party intends coming on Tuesday, which will be before our men get their uniforms. Some of our men will have to fly to the woods that day, as the rags they have on them will render it impossible for them to be seen by their friends."[21] In the end, the visit was cancelled out of respect for the soldiers. An editorial printed on June 10 confirms Brown's information:

> *Among the sufferers by the red tape formality and slow movements of the Military Canal Board, the Oswego Regiment occupies a prominent place. The regiment was formed early and, according to all rules of fairness, should have taken precedence receiving arms and uniforms. Yet the men have been kept there week after week, hoping against hope, and up to this day, no equipments have been furnished them. Since the Oswego boys have been upon the ground, shoeless and almost trowserless* [sic], *the Rochester and Syracuse regiments have been marched to the seat of war. The Oswego boys, on the ground longer than any of them, turn out in ragged trowsers* [sic] *and with no more than arms enough to mount guard. The consequences of this favoritism and delay are beginning to be felt. It is not in human nature to endure such treatment forever. The Oswego boys have borne with neglect week after week, still hoping to obtain their arms and uniforms. But they do not come. It seems probable that this long neglect will disband as gallant a regiment as ever answered the call of their country. Dissatisfaction is now openly expressed, and if the uniforms do not arrive this week, we may look for at least two hundred desertions.*[22]

On June 13, Colonel Henry Warner Slocum of the 127th (Auburn) Regiment refused uniforms sent to his men, declaring that the soldiers deserved better. Perhaps this is the reason why the Oswego troops did not receive theirs on June 12 as predicted. A short article states that the men were to have obtained their uniforms on June 11, "but [n]o arms have yet been issued—not even to drill a squad with—and our troops have yet to learn how to load and fire a musket."[23] In fact, the first uniforms did not arrive until June 20:

> *The Oswego Regiment to-day received uniforms for three companies, and it is expected that this evening will reveal to the gaze of both the Oswego and Union regiments enough army blue to well and properly clothe every man, and I can assure you that when the men shall have been donned with the long-looked-for apparel, a shout will be sent up unequaled by the war-whoops of the Six Nations. The inexcusable delay in clothing the Oswego Regiment has occasioned much dissatisfaction, but since the red tape has been finally cut, the boys stand ready to be forgiving. With good uniform*[s], *good rations and good discipline, the Oswegos now rank inferior to none.*[24]

Finally, the moment arrived for the regiment to leave Elmira. On July 2, the troops embarked by train for Washington, D.C., by way of Baltimore. Contemporary accounts report that they marched through the latter city with fixed bayonets to emphasize the strength of Union forces. Acting as a buffer for Union troops retreating from the disastrous and bloody first battle of Bull Run, they did picket duty for nineteen days without any protective cover. A letter written by S.H. Brown from Arlington Heights, Virginia, records the situation: "Our men are enjoying themselves, as far as camp life is concerned, better than they did during the nineteen days we were on picket duty, sleeping on the 'cold, cold ground.' But if we could have our tents, which now shelter us, we would much rather remain on the advance."[25] At the time of the retreat from Bull Run, the Twenty-fourth was the only organized force between the Confederates and the city of Washington.[26]

It is not my intent to retell the history of the Twenty-fourth Regiment but rather to show how its activities contributed to William Adriance's tale. As mentioned above, Edwin Huntington testified that Adriance complained considerably about his affliction while at Upton's Hill, where accommodations were primitive and lacking in appropriate sanitation. The change from the steamy summer weather to the cold and damp of autumn and winter undoubtedly worsened Adriance's pain. Despite health problems, however, he seems to have been able to carry out his duties, for in January 1862, he was promoted to sergeant major of Company B.

War began in earnest for the Twenty-fourth in the spring of 1862. Ordered to Bristol (also called Bristoe or Bristow) Station in the early part of April, the soldiers remained there for a week, during which time there occurred a snowstorm lasting three days. Parker O. Wright, a soldier in the Twenty-fourth, described it thus: "You do not forget 'Bristow Station' with three days' snowstorm and the wierd [*sic*] sight as you peeked out of your tent and saw the snow-capped mounds as though the balance of your comrades were all in a long, long sleep."[27]

Adriance's complaints about his rheumatism while at Bristol Station probably increased during the next few weeks. After first marching to Warrenton and Warrenton Junction, the troops slogged on to Cattlett's Station. On the morning of April 23, 1862, the regiment, together with other outfits belonging to the Army of the Potomac, set out for Fredericksburg to seize enemy stores and destroy bridges across the Rappahannock:

> *The march was begun. It was thirty-four miles. The weather was hot, and several of the men and horses were prostrated with sun stroke. Twenty miles without stopping was the first record, and then the order was given for a half of one hour to await orders and that the men might prepare themselves something to eat. Many were too tired after tramping in the hot sun with overcoats, knapsacks, blankets, haversacks and guns on their shoulders to give any attention to preparing coffee and they dropped down to the ground to rest. That the troops might be hurried to the front, they were ordered to pile knapsacks and overcoats at the side of the road and leave a guard to protect them. Then the cavalry took the long ropes with which their horses were tied while in camp and, fastening them to the pommels of their saddles, passed them back to the infantry and started away at a gallop, the men running behind. When the infantrymen became too exhausted to run further, the horses were turned about and went back to meet other troops, who were coming up at a double quick, and took a fresh supply in tow. In that way, they got up to where the rebels had barricaded the road. There was a sharp fight.*[28]

The extreme heat, heavy packs and a forced march of thirty-four miles, some of it on the end of a rope attached to a galloping horse, must have taken its toll on William Adriance. And more forced marching was at hand. The Union forces entered the small village of Falmouth on April 17, 1862, after seventeen hours on the road. It was as a result of this feat that General Marsena R. Patrick, "who, going through their camp, and finding everything arranged in military order, bestowed upon them the name of the 'Iron Brigade.'"[29] Falmouth is important for regimental history, as it was the first time the Twenty-fourth participated in an operation calculated to drive the Confederate forces across the Rappahannock River.

During the period covering April to early August, the Twenty-fourth marched hither and yon in Virginia, usually without much contact with the enemy. But all that was to change in August, when General John Pope's campaign began. Between August 22 and August 30, the regiment took part in battles at the Rappahannock River, Sulphur Springs, Gainesville, Groveton and (Second) Bull Run, losing 237 officers and men either to death or wounds. Although the Oswego boys fought bravely, Pope's campaign was a failure.

The fighting on Friday, August 29 (Groveton), and Saturday, August 30 (Second Bull Run), was especially savage:

> *The regiment came under fire about dusk on Friday, the first movement of the brigade to which it was attached being ordered by Gen.* [Irvin] *McDowell to pursue the rebels, who he supposed to be retreating. Darkness had now set in, and the brigades soon found themselves in a trap, and good fortune alone saved them from utter annihilation. They suddenly found themselves between two lines of the rebels, with artillery on both flanks and a battery in front. A murderous fire was opened on them. On Saturday, the regiment was under artillery fire the entire forenoon and came into the infantry action about 3 o'clock in the afternoon. This day a fatal charge was made by our gallant boys which resulted in another mortality list of nearly 200 men. The regiment was stationed in a piece of woods and were ordered to charge the rebels, who were stationed on a high railroad track. To accomplish this, it was necessary to cross an open field, a distance of about 100 yards. The brave 24th after receiving the order gave a cheer and gallantly dashed for the embankment. While crossing this field, the men fell rapidly, and upon arriving at the railroad track, it was ascertained their task had been fruitless, as the enemy in immense numbers were stationed upon and beyond it. Orders were given to retreat, and the remnant of the 24th, keeping along the base of the embankment, obtained the shelter of the woods again with its ranks sadly shattered by their gallant but futile charge.*[30]

The low morale of the troops following Bull Run can be discerned from an excerpt of a letter Joseph W. Cooley, a member of Company B, sent to his brother John. Dated October 5, 1862, the letter records how Cooley reacted to his regiment's defeat: "The next morning, I cried like a baby to think that Hatch's brigade had been whipped. What will Oswego say that the Twenty-Fourth is whipped?"[31]

After the Battle of Groveton, William Adriance was promoted to second lieutenant and transferred to Company A. It appears he had been angling for a promotion for several months, perhaps hoping for a less physically stressful position. He had supporters, as is revealed in a letter of recommendation from author Benson John Lossing to Governor Edwin D. Morgan. Lossing (1813–1891) was a well-known author and engraver who met Henry Adriance while hawking his books in New York City. The cordial relationship between Lossing and the Adriance family is demonstrated by the fact that Henry and Mary named their third daughter Alice Lossing Adriance.

Lossing's letter says much about Adriance's character and background:

> *There is a well educated, fine figured and brave young man of 30, named William Henry Adriance, in the 24th (Oswego) Regiment, who fought bravely during the late 3 days' battles in Virginia and who asks for a lieutenancy. He is the son of an old friend, a bookseller in Oswego. He was recommended for promotion by now Col. D.C.* [Dewitt Clinton] *Littlejohn several months ago. His father has written to the adjutant-general on the subject. The adjutant of the 24th, now sick at home, speaks highly of his bravery in the late battles. His father, knowing that I know you personally, has asked me by letter to write to you on his behalf. I do so cheerfully. I have known the young soldier from his infancy, and I believe that a promotion would be of essential service to the public, as his talents and personal* [illegible] *raise him naturally above the ranks to a position of wider usefulness.*[32]

The regiment moved to Centerville, where it engaged in more fighting against the Rebels before retreating again to Upton's Hill. A contemporary account recalled, "A train of wagons and ambulances sent out on Thursday to the battle-field at Centerville, returned on Sunday, having on board some 600 or 700 wounded. It is said that some of the wounded remained three days on the battle-field without food. If this be so, it is the most inexcusable and inhuman outrage yet perpetrated, and one that should never be allowed to occur again."[33]

The situation was about to change, however, thanks to the heroic efforts of Dr. Jonathan Letterman (1824–1872), who was designated medical director of the Army of the Potomac in June 1862. Letterman realized that an organized ambulance corps, developed in a military hierarchy, was required to save lives of the wounded and ill. Prior to his reforms, civilians were accustomed to driving the wagons bearing the stretchers, and they were generally unwilling to recover wounded men while bullets and artillery balls were whizzing around them. Their replacements, however, were untrained and often unscrupulous soldiers. At the Battle of Groveton (August 29), "it was discovered that three thousand wounded were left on the field for three days and six hundred were left for a week. This was because the ambulance drivers who replaced the civilians picked the pockets of the wounded, stole alcohol from the medical supplies and left the injured to die. As a result of these and other scandals, Letterman's system was gradually adopted by all Union armies." [34] For example, by the time the Battle of Antietam was fought on September 17, 1862, "the performance of Letterman's ambulance corps had improved significantly. Stretcher-bearers first carried the wounded to primary stations and then loaded them into ambulances to be transported to the field hospital on a fixed schedule with regular stops en route."[35] The ambulance corps' efficiency reached a peak by the time of the Battle of Gettysburg in July 1863: "In his report, Letterman added that Surgeon John McNulty, medical director of the Twelfth Corps, noted, 'It is with extreme satisfaction that I can assure you that the wounded were removed from the field, sheltered, fed, and dressed their wounds within six hours after the battle ended, and to have every capital operation performed within 24 hours after injury was received.'"[36]

The Twenty-fourth Regiment saw action at South Mountain on September 14 and at Antietam on September 17, but the next important operation for Lieutenant Adriance was the Battle of Fredericksburg, December 13, 1862, since his military papers reveal he was on detached duty with the ambulance corps from November 1862 until April 1863.

Pressured by President Abraham Lincoln, who desperately needed a victory to bolster his public approval, General Ambrose Burnside reluctantly took control of the Union army. After weeks of miscommunications, delays and failure to prepare properly, the Union soldiers were destined to become just so many targets for the well-entrenched Rebels, who held the heights to the south of the city. As the fog rose on Saturday, December 13, General Robert E. Lee could see the entire Union army from his vantage point. Over 100,000 troops were about to risk their lives in a futile gesture. The gory details of the battle need not be rehearsed here; many others have done that, including the participants themselves. My reason for describing this battle is to demonstrate the bravery of members of the ambulance corps, especially Lieutenant Adriance, while under fire.

As the Union forces began their march across the plain toward the Rebel stronghold, hidden on a hill called Marysheight, they immediately came under cannon fire from three sides that killed or maimed hundreds. According to witnesses, men were decapitated, disemboweled or repeatedly wounded.

Soldiers were left leaderless when their officers, hoping to encourage them, led the charge and were mowed down. Those lucky enough to reach the base of Marysheight were massacred by 2,500 Confederate soldiers hiding behind a stone wall partway up the hill.[37] A letter written by William B. Gillespie of the U.S. Signal Corps described the devastation:

> *Although they fought until after dark, they had gained nothing of importance and lost heavily—what number is not yet ascertained. I should not be surprised if it reached six or seven thousand killed and wounded. The wounded have been gathered up and taken to hospitals prepared for them in churches and houses in Fredericksburgh. Many of the dead still lie upon the field, our men being unable to get them on account of their being near the enemy's earthworks, who open fire at any attempt of our men to obtain them.*[38]

One witness reported that dead Union soldiers lay three deep at some points.[39]

The battle was doubly dangerous for the ambulance corps. Not only were the men in the line of fire as they tried to remove the wounded and dead from the battlefield, but they also had no weapons with which to defend themselves. Thus, they, too, became fodder for Confederate cannon and sharpshooters. Lieutenant Melvin R. Baldwin, under whom Adriance served at the Battle of Fredericksburg, wrote a report on this operation to his commander, Captain B. Hutchinson, on December 27. In this letter, he named Adriance as the commander of the First Brigade ambulance corps. All through the day, the men of the ambulance corps picked up the wounded, delivered them to field stations and sent them to general hospitals in the rear. Baldwin wrote, "Sunday morning, I returned to the division hospital with ten two-horse ambulances. At the same time, Lieutenant Adriance, in charge of stretcher-bearers, was relieved by Lieut. C. Kellogg of the third Brigade, the former having become exhausted from the severity of the labors devolving upon him." Apparently, Adriance had spent the entire night overseeing efforts to remove an estimated thirteen thousand wounded and dead Union soldiers from the battlefield.[40] Instead of the victory Lincoln desired, a great tragedy occurred, leaving many Unionists wondering if the war could be won. Although details are not available, one can guess the state of Lieutenant Adriance's health at the conclusion of his herculean effort on behalf of the wounded.

The Twenty-fourth Regiment, reserved from the Battle of Fredericksburg, had done picket duty and was among the last to recross the Rappahannock when Burnside retreated. After participating in several more skirmishes, the regiment went into winter quarters at Belle Plain.[41] From Adriance's records, it is evident that he was on detached service until April 1863, although exact locations cannot be ascertained. By this time, his regiment was awaiting the end of its service. In May, the troops were transported to Elmira to begin mustering out. Their official discharge date was May 29, 1863.

As the time for the Twenty-fourth to return to Oswego approached, local newspapers were full of stories about the preparations. To celebrate, the entire community banded together. On June 1, the *Commercial Times* reported, "They are now in Elmira, and arrangements have been made to have intelligence at the earliest moment their homeward movement is determined on. On their arrival at Syracuse, the city bells will be rung for half an hour; and as the train approaches Oswego, a national salute will be fired from near the depot."[42] Other plans included a march through the streets on a circuitous route around the downtown area. The entire regiment was invited to ride in wagons for the parade. A patriotic program, complete with songs, speeches and prayers, furnished the entertainment. To finish off the big welcome-home party, the "ladies" of the city served a sumptuous dinner at the Doolittle Hotel. While no mention of him is available, it must be surmised that William Adriance was among the returnees. One person who was almost certainly awaiting a glimpse of him was Lydia Gertrude Lord, William's future wife. How long William and Lydia had known each other is uncertain, but she once said that she had become acquainted with him four years prior to their wedding, which would have made her approximately twenty years old.[43]

Lydia was the second child and second daughter of Reverend Lord and his wife, Laura. Although it is known she was born on March 2, 1839, her birthplace is a mystery. On one census, she reportedly had been born in the town of Genoa. Another source claims that she was born in Gilberts Mills, Schroeppel, Oswego County. Yet another citation gives Cayuga County as her birthplace. Nevertheless, she spent most of her formative years in the town of Scriba. As the offspring of a minister, Lydia almost certainly had a more thorough education than other girls. In fact, the 1855 Scriba census states that she and older sister, Sarah, were teachers.

Lydia and William were married on September 30, 1863, at the family home by Reverend Mason Gallagher.[44] Married life for the young couple must have been difficult from the outset on account of William's health. Lydia's sister, Mary Adeline Fletcher, described his condition thus: "I saw [William Adriance] immediately after his discharge. He was then suffering from rheumatism and troubled with shortness of breath. He looked bad and complained of his back and joints. He had pain in his breast and around his heart."[45] Another sister, Catherine Pease, deposed, "I remember he returned from the war in poor health. He was lame and complaining of rheumatism[;] at times, he could hardly get about. The rheumatic trouble seemed to affect him all over. I have known him to get up nights, as he could not rest on account of pain. He suffered more or less with the rheumatism during all the time he remained here [in Oswego]."[46] Also furnishing evidence was Joshua Miner, who stated, "During the time [Adriance] remained here, he complained of rheumatism in his back. He would have attacks frequently. He laid his trouble to taking cold from exposure in the Army."[47]

Poor health meant that Adriance had trouble finding work. Gone was his bookstore. He attempted upholstery, working for David Sinclair on West First Street.[48] Lydia said many years later that William tried to help her father with farm chores but found the exertion too taxing. Money was tight. In fact, William reported absolutely no income in 1863. In contrast, his father said he had an income of $838 that year.[49]

William and Lydia's first child, Henry "Harry" Chapman Adriance, was born on October 24, 1864. Little did they know that this boy would become a Medal of Honor winner for bravery in the Boxer Rebellion. As the Adriance family welcomed its newest member, the war continued to rage, and more men were needed to fill the ranks of the dead and the discharged. Lincoln called for a fourth draft, and on November 26, 1864, the War Department ordered Major General Winfield Scott Hancock (1824–1886), a hero of the Battle of Gettysburg and later a candidate for U.S. president, to form a veteran corps to be known as the First Veteran Volunteer Corps. News of this organization was disseminated widely, and it was hoped that twenty thousand veterans would reenlist.[50] The goal was to fill the nine regiments by the end of February, but recruiting continued into March.

The incentives to enlist were appealing. Upon mustering in, the soldier received a bounty of $300 plus an extra $100 and local bounties. Opportunities existed to sign on for one, two or even three years. In addition to the money, the recruit would be issued the best weapon available and would be permitted to retain it upon discharge "as the honorable testimony of his faithful service in the national army."[51]

Adriance was qualified to serve in this new corps because he had seen active duty for two years and was therefore immune to the draft. Given the state of his health, however, it is hard to understand how he passed the physical. Dr. J.A. Murdock pronounced him fit for duty on March 15, 1865, and he was mustered into Company F, Eighth Regiment, USVV, that same day. Adriance enlisted in the town of Volney, although city directories showed him living in Oswego. No matter how he managed it, he and Lydia were $400 richer (at least on paper)—money they desperately needed. Too bad fate intervened.

Adriance left for Washington, D.C., headquarters of the unit, on March 16. A month later, General Lee surrendered to General Grant at Appomattox. While it is impossible to say for certain how Adriance reacted to the prospect of staying in the army once the war was finished, he probably was not very happy. Nevertheless, on May 6, he was promoted to corporal. Whatever pleasure he derived from his promotion was soon shattered by news that his father had died on Sunday, May 7, after a brief but painful illness. His obituary described him thus: "Mr. Adriance was one of our oldest and most respected citizens. He had been engaged in mercantile pursuits during a long time amongst us and had borne the reputation of a strictly honest man. He was an active and consistent Christian. His life and death witnessed the deep sincerity of his professions, and he has left his children an honored name."[52] Also published in that edition of the *Daily Palladium* was an invitation for the members of Oswego Lodge #127 and Frontier Lodge #422 Free and Accepted Masons to attend the funeral of their "Brother Henry Adriance" on Tuesday at 1:00 p.m.

While we await Corporal Adriance's arrival in Oswego, let us take a more detailed look at the family, beginning with Papa Henry. A bookseller in New York City, he was also affiliated with the Mechanics' School, serving at one time as secretary of the school committee. Henry, a religious man, became involved in the Oswego County Bible Society, at one time serving as treasurer.[53] In his will, Henry left to each of his daughters "a family Bible bound in rich, blue Turkey Morocco super extra" with the hope "that it may be to them the lamp of life and the wisdom of God unto salvation." He was active in politics and community affairs. In 1850, he was the chair of a committee charged with organizing the annual Fourth of July celebration.[54]

Henry's wife, Mary Eliza Beach, was born in New York City on March 20, 1810, the daughter of William Beach (1785–ante 1850) and Hester Conkling (1789–ante 1860). Beach was a shoemaker. In the 1850 census for New York City Ward 10, Hester, a widow aged sixty-one, was living with her son Martin M. Beach, MD (ca. 1825–1874) and his wife, Sarah (?–1884).[55] The Adriances' second child, Mary Eliza (1835–1874), appears to have been a thoroughly competent woman. Directory entries and census records reveal that she worked in the family bookstore. After her father's death, she assumed the bulk of the responsibility for proving the will, since her mother was ill. She sent the following letter, dated June 14, 1865, to Surrogate Judge Timothy Skinner: "I received the enclosed 'renunciation' this morning. Mr. [Lawrence] Sinclair has consented to act as an appraiser. I have not yet seen Mr. Brown. My mother has failed much since last Saturday...was very low indeed last night. Her symptoms are rather better this morning."

Mary sold the business in 1870, in which year the census shows her living with relatives in New York City. Apparently, she returned to Oswego briefly, as the 1872–73 city directory lists her as working as a postal clerk and boarding at 92 West Fifth Street. She might have stayed in Oswego except for failing health:

> *The friends of Miss Mary Adriance, of this city, will learn with the deepest regret that she lies very low with the consumption at the residence of her aunt, Mrs. Charles Gennet* [Elizabeth Ayraud Adriance, Henry's sister], *in Richmond, VA. Miss Adriance's health commenced to fail last summer, and it was but too evident to her friends that she was marked for an early victim to that most insidious of all diseases. She has grown weaker gradually, until all hope is over, and her friends must be prepared to hear the worst at any moment.*[56]

Several days later, her obituary appeared:

> *The citizens of Oswego will be pained to learn of the death of Miss Mary E. Adriance, of this city, in Richmond, VA., yesterday. Miss Adriance was the eldest daughter of the late Henry Adriance, for many years one of our best known and most highly respected businessmen. She was a lady of rare intelligence and of a most sincere and unpretending Christianity. All through life, Miss Adriance had been marked for her womanly virtues and Christian graces. She was a devoted and faithful daughter, upon whom her father and mother leaned in their declining years, and she never failed them. She was the most devoted, affectionate and kind of sisters, and in all the relations of a true woman's life, she was an intelligent and always highly respected lady.*[57]

An effort was made to bring her body home to be buried alongside her parents in Riverside, but her uncle wrote to Mayor Benjamin Doolittle informing him that it had been Mary's last wish to be buried in Hollywood Cemetery in Richmond, Virginia. Her grave is located in the Gennet plot and is graced with a lovely tombstone.[58]

Mary Adriance is buried in historic Hollywood Cemetery in Richmond, Virginia. *Courtesy of Hollywood Cemetery.*

In 1836, the Adriances were blessed with a third child, a son they named John Alfred. This boy met with a tragic end on May 7, 1842:

> *The coroner held an inquest at the house of Mr. Henry Adriance, No. 198 Fulton street, on the body of his son John A., a very interesting lad, about*

> *five years and a half old, who was killed by being run over by an omnibus in Broadway while he was attempting to pass from the east to the west side of the street...having been in company with an elder brother to a hair-dresser's. It appeared from the evidence that the omnibus was proceeding at a very moderate pace and that the accident was occasioned by the lad avoiding a cart when the omnibus struck him and the fire wheel passed over his body.* [He] *died in half an hour afterwards.*[59]

The child identified as "an elder brother" could be only William Henry.

Henry and Mary's next child, born in 1840, was named Thomas Mesnard. Unfortunately, the infant died soon after he was born: "On Wednesday morning, THOMAS MAINARD [MESNARD], infant son of Henry and Mary E. Adriance. Funeral this afternoon at 4 o'clock, from 198 Fulton St."[60]

Sarah Gonsalves Adriance, born 1841, was the last child born in New York City. Her first and middle names were honorific for her aunt Sarah and uncle Emanuel Gonsalves. She died in Oswego on March 17, 1849, at the age of seven and was buried in the family plot in Riverside Cemetery, where her tombstone can still be seen.

Alice Lossing Adriance was born in Oswego in 1843. We have already discussed the source for her middle name. Much of Alice's adult life is shadowy, but it is known that she married Edwin Henry Hiller (1846–1906) in Denver, Colorado. The *Ryerson Genealogy* mistakenly identifies him as Edward Miller. He, too, is a shadowy character. He was born in Sharon Springs, Schoharie County, New York, the son of Charles and Julia Hiller. Hiller, a businessman, was involved in several lawsuits, one of which went all the way to the Colorado Supreme Court in 1888 and hinted at corruption.[61] In 1897, he was sued in California. After spending time mining for gold in Alaska, he died in Seattle, Washington, on September 4, 1906.

As for Alice, it was probably a blessing that she died in 1874. It spared her the agony and humiliation of living with a husband who may or may not have been a charlatan. The couple had two children, one of whom died in 1873 and the other in 1875.[62]

Gertrude Adriance, Henry and Mary's seventh child, was born in 1846. Little can be said of this girl except that her tombstone records she was "3 yrs, 11 mos & 7 days" old when she died in Oswego in 1850.

Cornelia Temple Adriance was born in 1848, the same year in which Oswego was incorporated as a city. When Henry died, she was a minor who had to have a guardian to protect her interests. Since her mother was disqualified from this position, Surrogate Judge Timothy Skinner appointed Brainard Nelson to act on her behalf. Five years later, Cornelia and her older sister Alice, both giving their occupation as dressmakers in the 1870 census, were living with Aaron and Margaret Wentworth Gennet in Binghamton, Broome County. Aaron and Charles Gennet, with whom Mary was living at the time of her death, were brothers. Charles was married to Elizabeth Ayraud Adriance (1811–1902), sister of Henry Adriance and thus aunt of the four girls.

Before continuing with Cornelia's story, let us turn to the youngest child of Henry and Mary Adriance, Julia Louisa (1851–1932). She was also a minor when her father died, and Nelson was appointed her guardian. Where the two resided after their parents died can only be surmised, but perhaps they were with either William and Lydia or Mary Eliza. In 1870, when Mary was living in New York City and Cornelia and Alice in Binghamton, Julia resided in Oswego, attending school and boarding with Harmon and Alice Hamilton.

It is at this point that, for some as-yet-unknown reason, the younger sisters' lives converged again. Edwin Hiller married Alice in Denver in 1870, although we do not know how the couple met or how the sisters got to Colorado. Hiller found work at the Colorado National Bank. He was also involved in the affairs of St. John's Episcopal Church and the most likely person to introduce Julia to her future husband, Reverend Walter Howard Moore. Born in Warren, Rhode Island, on December 18, 1844, he was the son of Thomas and Abby Wheaton Moore. After being ordained a priest, he spent six years at St. John's Episcopal Church in Denver. He married Julia on January 28, 1875. A notice published in an unidentified Denver newspaper announced that Moore and Julia Adriance were married at Trinity Memorial Chapel on Twenty-sixth Street. The bride was "escorted by a brother-in-law E.H. Hiller."[63] Of course, by this time, Hiller was a widower, as Alice had died the previous year.

By 1876, Reverend Moore and Julia had been transferred to Napa, California. Their first child, Thomas Alexander, was born there on August 4, 1876. He died of pneumonia in Oak Park, Illinois, on April 11, 1923. Alice Adriance Moore was born in Aurora, Illinois, on January 29, 1879, but died on March 6. Twins Walter Adriance Moore and George Seymour Adriance Moore were born on February 23, 1880. Walter died in April 1880, but George reached adulthood and, like his father, became an Episcopal priest. In 1918, Reverend Moore registered for the draft and listed his mother, with whom he was residing, as his next of kin. Like his father, he had several churches. For example, in 1920, he was in Coldwater, Michigan.[64] In 1942, Reverend Moore was required to register for the "old man's draft." He died in Chicago on November 4, 1942, and was buried with his mother and siblings in Greenwood Cemetery in Decatur, Illinois. The couple's youngest child, Francis "Frank" Michael, was born in 1882 and died in 1953.

Reverend Walter Moore's career continued until his death. He and Julia were last posted at St. Luke's Church in South Glastonbury, Connecticut. According to his death certificate, it was here on May 11, 1917, that he died of septicemia and gangrene in the right foot. He was buried in the Old Church Cemetery in South Glastonbury, where his monument can still be seen. His demise explains why Julia was living with George in 1918. She died in 1932.

While Julia's movements are easily traced, the same cannot be said of Cornelia after 1870, although a few tempting tidbits do exist. For example, a Miss Nellie Adriance of Denver, Colorado, joined the Colorado Teachers' Association at its first meeting in 1876.[65] The name Nellie, of course, is not Cornelia, but as terms of endearment go, it is not implausible. Secondly, the Decatur Post Office reported a letter waiting for Nellie F. Adriance on July 9, 1879.[66] Although the middle initial was given as "F," it could easily have been misread, since "F" and "T" were often written similarly. Someone may have known that Julia was living in the area (she and Walter were transferred to St. John's Church, Decatur, in 1879) and took a chance that Cornelia was there, too. Because of the date, Cornelia/Nellie might have been spending her summer vacation with Julia. A third glimpse into Cornelia's movements can be found in a Denver City Directory. Nellie T. Adriance was listed as a teacher at the Stout School.[67] I conclude, therefore, that Cornelia Temple Adriance, Miss Nellie F. Adriance and Nellie T. Adriance were one and the same person.

Since Cornelia is not listed on any census records, the years between 1882 and 1886 are cloaked in silence. She died on January 12, 1887, at Julia's home in Chicago. According to the certificate, the cause of death was tuberculosis. The record also revealed that she had been a resident of Illinois for six months, which roughly translates into June 1886, or the end of the school year. Cornelia's funeral was held at her brother-in-law's church, Calvary, on January 14.[68] She was buried in an unmarked grave in Mount Greenwood Cemetery.

Let us now return to Corporal William H. Adriance, who has arrived in Oswego for his father's funeral. One wonders if he was in for a surprise when the will was read, because he inherited nothing. His army records show that he did not receive any of his bounty until June 6, and not sharing in his father's estate (especially with a wife and child to support) must have been a hard pill to swallow. On May 16, he returned by rail to Washington, D.C., where he was stationed at Camp Stoneman.

After Henry died, his wife and daughter took over the bookstore. Advertisements in the local newspapers first appeared under Mrs. Adriance's name, but in late June, classifieds showed that Miss Mary Eliza had assumed the business. Mrs. Adriance died on July 19, 1865, and was buried next to her husband in Riverside Cemetery.

For a second time, William was forced to return home for a funeral. According to the two transportation requisitions found among his military papers, he stayed for approximately two weeks and returned to duty on August 5. If he was unhappy about being forced to remain in the army after the war had ended, he must have been made even more so when he had to leave his sister to care for the family while he cooled his heels in a Washington, D.C. military camp. It may have been on the trip back to Camp Stoneman that he hatched his plan to force the army to discharge him early.

The old adage says, "The squeaky wheel gets the grease," and William's campaign to escape the clutches of the U.S. Army provides a wonderful example. His military record shows that he deserted on May 18, two days

The Adriance family plot contains Henry, Mary, Sarah, Gertrude, Alfred "Allie" and Lydia Lord Adriance. *Author's collection.*

after returning from his father's funeral. He was returned to camp on May 20. Apparently, this action did not result in the desired discharge, because on September 29, he deserted again. He either returned freely or was arrested. On October 6, he was reduced in rank to private upon recommendation of his commanding officer, Captain Maxwell. He was tried by court-martial on November 10, sentenced to two weeks in the guardhouse and ordered to forfeit one month's pay. What occurred between November 10 and November 28 is murky, but on that date, Adriance was discharged from the service based on Special Order 619 issued on November 27 "by order of the Secretary of War."[69] Military correspondence suggests that someone in the background was helping him. One document states that Adriance's discharge took place "by way of favor."[70] Could his guardian angel have been Edwin Stanton himself? While no link has been made between them, it is curious that William's commanding officer, Lieutenant Colonel W. L. Monk, was questioned as to why he had erased the words "no objection to his being reenlisted is known to exist" from the original discharge.[71] Monk replied to Major R. Chandler, assistant adjutant general, the same day: "His company commander informs me that he has acted the part of a shirk since he [Captain Maxwell] took command of the company—frequently boasting that he was making more than colonel's pay (bounty &c) and with the aid of a certain friend he could receive a discharge at any time."[72] Response to Monk's letter was swift. He was informed that his reason for altering the discharge paper was inappropriate and ordered to issue a new one to be directed to headquarters immediately.[73] On top of tampering with the discharge papers, Augur accused Monk of refusing to permit William to retain his weapon: "Pvt. Adrianse [*sic*] also complains that he has not been permitted to avail himself of the privilage [*sic*] granted to soldiers honorably discharged of retaining his arms &c in Gen'l Ord. No. 101 from War Department May 13, 1865."

William had appealed to General Hancock for his arms, writing, "General, I have this day been discharged from the 8th Regt, 1st A[rmy] C[orps], by order of the Secretary of War and was denied the privilege of taking my gun by the captain. I would respectfully ask if I am not entitled to the gun, as it was understood when I enlisted that the men were to have them when discharged." General Dent was ordered to "call upon the officer [Monk] responsible for a full explanation of his refusal to comply."[74]

The very next day, Monk sent the following missive to Brevet Captain G.E. Henry: "In compliance with instructions received this date, I have the honor to forward a new discharge—properly filled out—for Private Adriance...

and would state that as regards his retaining the arms issued to him, I have no authority to allow him that priviledge [*sic*], not having as yet received Gen'l Order No. 101 from War Dept. May 13, 1865." Monk added that the only information he had obtained about retaining arms was contained in Circular No. 5 from headquarters, dated October 7, 1865, a copy of which he enclosed. This document clearly set forth the classes of soldiers entitled to their arms if they were discharged before their term of service expired: commissioned staff officers, veteran musicians and non-veteran musicians "honorably discharged before or at the expiration of their terms of enlistment."

The case dragged on until mid-December, when now–private citizen Adriance, whose address was given as Washington, D.C., received a letter from Assistant Adjutant General Finley Anderson: "In reply to your communication of the 28th…requesting information whether you are entitled to your gun, I have to inform you that your letter has been referred to the War Department and received back with the decision that you are not entitled to the gun unless you were discharged by reason of expiration of your term of service or because your services were no required."[75] This decision could only have intensified the misery of a man who had endured so much pain that year. It was time to go home.

No exact date can be fixed for the unhappy man's return to Oswego, but since Clara Ione arrived in September 1866, he likely arrived in late December or early January. Nor has any evidence surfaced for 1866, although the city directory lists him as living on East Sixth Street near Cayuga. Perhaps he helped his father-in-law on the farm in Scriba, and he may have assisted his sister in the bookstore. The city directories for 1867–68 and 1868–69 gave his occupation as clerk in the City Bookstore. During these years, he resided at 97 East Fifth Street. Since Mary Eliza was living at the family home on West Oneida Street, it is to be presumed that William and Lydia had established their own household. Nevertheless, the couple soon made a decision that would take them away from Oswego. They would head to the Pennsylvania oil fields to make their fortune.

The first successful oil well in Pennsylvania was drilled in Titusville in 1859. Soon, oil fields were popping up all over the western part of the state, one of them at Shamburg, which was considered a "boomtown" in 1868. Established by Dr. George Shamburg, principal owner of the Cherry Run Petroleum Company, it had a population of two thousand. William, Lydia, Henry and Clara were enumerated for the 1870 census in

This early photo of the Shamburg Oil Field emphasizes its rural atmosphere. *Courtesy of Drake Oil Museum.*

Shamburg. In the same year, Alfred John (sometimes called John Alfred or Allie) was born on July 12.

By 1873, Shamburg and its environs were deserted. Like everyone else, William and Lydia migrated to a supposedly richer territory. They appear on the 1880 census for Karns City, Butler County, where vast amounts of oil had been discovered in the 1860s and '70s. Their last child, Edward Seeley Adriance, was born there on February 1, 1880. Like his brother Henry, he would have a long, interesting and even bizarre life.

Moving did not free the family from financial difficulties or William from his physical ailments. Years later, when Lydia was applying for a widow's pension, acquaintances deposed about their knowledge of William's health. Helen Seeley testified, "I have often heard him speak of his exposure in the army and heard him say that the rheumatism which had settled in his back he had gotten while in the army. Often he could not get into bed himself but his wife had to get him in as best she could. I know when he had those spells of rheumatism in his back that [he] used a great deal of medicine. He never was a stout hearty man after I got acquainted with him. He was not able to stand hard work."[76] Joshua Miner, Sarah's husband, recalled, "During the time he remained here [in Oswego], he complained of rheumatism in his back. At times, he could hardly move about. He would have attacks frequently. He had not recovered when he left here. He laid his trouble to taking cold from exposure in the Army."[77]

Witnesses were unanimous in their descriptions of William's physical debility. Catherine Carter, a neighbor in Karns City, reported, "I know that he suffered a great deal with his back. At times, he would be so bad that he had to be helped to bed. I recollect one occasion seeing them carry him into the house, and his wife told me that he had fallen suddenly from pain in his back."[78] Kate (Pease) Dutcher, Lydia's sister, remembered, "We received letters from them after they went to the oil regions in which they stated they had to inject morphine in him on account of the severe pain from the rheumatism."[79] Edward Seeley, another Karns neighbor, recalled, "I recollect that a few weeks before his death, he was over to our house one day, and I noticed how white he was; his face was pale as a dead man's. I recollect speaking to my wife at the time about it, and I also asked him how he felt, and [he] answered, 'None of the best.' He was a man who did not say much. He belonged to a good family—he had got down and could not get up and was rather reserved."[80] Seeley's remark contained more truth than he probably knew. The Adriance family was wealthy, and had he chosen to ask, William undoubtedly could have obtained a well-paying, less arduous occupation that would have lifted the family from the edge of poverty and, more importantly, extended his life. The only conclusion to be made is that he was too proud to ask for help.

William's unhappy life ended on March 29, 1885. According to testimony provided by several witnesses, he had been called into work at midnight to substitute for a sick worker. His task was to fill the coal car, push it to the station and then shovel the coal into the steam furnace pumping the oil. Orrin S. June, his supervisor, observing him working very quickly, told him to slow down. He later recounted:

> *About an hour after he came on duty, a car was run back to the coal house, and he loaded the car. This car would hold about a ton of coal. After loading this car, he ran it into the bailey. I was explaining to him something about the working of the bailey when suddenly he fell over on his back. This was about 2:10 a.m. I did not see him fall. He was standing just a little behind me. I heard the sound and turned and saw him lying on his back. I think he was dead the minute after he fell.*[81]

June's report was echoed by that of oil producer Patrick R. Burke, who testified that he had known Adriance since 1873, when the veteran did odd jobs of a "light character" for him: "I never considered him a hearty stout man, and he was not able to heavy manual labor. There was something peculiar about his walk, yet I never inquired the cause. It was the general opinion at the time of his death that his death was caused by heart trouble of some kind and the occasion was the work which he did at the time, as the work was perhaps too much for him."[82] By the time depositions were being solicited for Lydia's pension, however, the attending physician, Dr. Harper, had died. When asked, no one present that evening could remember what he said was the cause of death. The local newspaper noted, "W.H. Adriance, fireman at the Karns City pump station, dropped dead from apoplexy Sunday."[83] He was buried in Bear Creek Cemetery in Fairview Township, Butler County, near Petrolia, Pennsylvania. A marker provided under an act to purchase stones for Union soldiers from 1879 to 1903 points out his grave. He was fifty-two years old.

How did Lydia react to this tragedy? Luther Stone, who arrived shortly after Adriance fell, told her the sad news: "When I notified his wife of his death, she said, 'It was nothing more than she expected from him.'"[84] Many years later, when applying for a widow's pension, Lydia pooh-poohed the notion that William had overexerted himself and thereby caused his death: "I was never satisfied the way the evidence formerly went in; it stated he was loading a car & that the exertion killed him. The car would hold between 10 and 15 bushels [of] coal and was run a distance of 30 feet on tracks. His work was light—a boy of 14 years of age could do it."[85] She clung to the theory that the war had been the primary cause of his sudden demise, possibly worried she would be denied her pension if the government determined that her husband's disability was not war-related.

Comments by two special examiners offer poignant perspectives on Adriance. Writing to the commissioner of pensions, J.N. Cutherton observed, "Soldier was a man of good family and above the average in intelligence and education. He had got to the foot of [the] ladder financially and found it impossible to mount, and this soured him just a little, and as a result, he kept aloof from complaining to his fellows. Soldier was a man of good habits, and death cannot be laid [to] any bad habit."[86] S. Hotaling wrote the following to the commissioner: "From his return from the Army and up to the time he left Oswego, his life is a blank to the people. I could find no one that had any recollection of him. Many that he associated with are dead, [and] others have forgotten him. I could get no evidence except from relatives. It is proper to remark they are all first-class people."[87]

Lydia quickly left Karns City. She was listed in the 1886 Oswego City Directory as living at 73 East Cayuga Street. Clara, a dressmaker, and John A., a clerk, boarded with her. Presumably, six-year-old Edward lived there, too. There is no listing for Henry, but by the time the 1888 directory was published, he was listed as living with Lydia and working as a brakeman on the railroad.

Lydia obtained a pension for herself and her two minor sons, John and Edward. Records show that between March 1885 and March 28, 1886, she collected eight dollars per month plus two dollars for each child per month. After March 29, 1886, Lydia received twelve dollars per month plus two dollars for each boy. When John turned sixteen in July 1886, his pension fund closed. Edward would continue receiving money until July 11, 1896.

In 1890, Lydia applied for a pension increase under the new act. Initially rejected, she eventually won her case: "Mrs. L.G. Adriance, formerly of this city, now of Syracuse, has received a back pension amounting to $1,000 and will hereafter receive $12 per month."[88]

The Adriances' son John died a gruesome death on August 29, 1892. At the time, he was working on the railroad in Oneida County:

> *An eyewitness related the facts to a* Times *reporter as follows: Adriance was a brakeman on train thirty, Washington Mills conductor, and was making up the train to go West. Adriance was attending to the rear end of the train making a coupling. In walking to the place where the coupling was to be made, he ran his foot between the guard rail and the rail proper and signaled the train to go ahead. Then he tried to pull his foot out little thinking it was so firmly fastened. When he saw he could not get his foot loose, he made a grab and caught hold of the passing box car, but his hold was not good, and he fell, striking on his face. The wheel of the car passed over his back, running the whole length of his body and crushing his head into an unrecognizable mass.*[89]

His body was brought to Oswego and buried in Riverside.[90]

Other changes were in store for the Adriance family. On May 14, 1890, Henry "Harry" Adriance married Helen Frances "Nellie" Gadbaw (1868–1954) in Scriba. The couple resided in Syracuse, where Henry worked on the railroad. Henry and Helen were the parents of two sons, George Louis (1891–1975) and Harold Allie (1894–1978). Lydia was also living in the Salt City. City directories reveal that she was running a boardinghouse and that her sister Mary A. (sometimes called Adeline Mary) Lord Fletcher (1843–1902) was in business with her.

Clara Ione married Charles Henry Evans, another railroad man, in 1893. Evans, a widower, resided in Lydia's boardinghouse before he and Clara were wed. They eventually moved to Buffalo, where he secured work with the Southern Railroad. The 1910 census put them at 26 Whitney Place with two sons, Charles Fay (1896–1970) and Carroll A. (1908–1976). A third child, Lydia A., was born in March 1898. She died on June 26, 1906, and her body was returned to Oswego for burial.[91]

Charles Henry Evans was Clara's husband. They were the parents of two boys and one girl. *Courtesy of Patricia Zwick.*

Dependent on her pension, Lydia had received an increase when she turned seventy, and she applied for a further increase when the law was amended to offer pensioners the sum of $50.00 per month. The proviso was that the widow must have been married to the veteran before his service in order to qualify. Since Lydia married Adriance in 1863, after his discharge from the Twenty-fourth Regiment, the government informed her that she did not qualify. Lydia had few records pertaining to her husband's second enlistment, but the problem was eventually resolved, and she began receiving her new allotment. As part of the search to locate evidence, a letter came to light indicating that William had not obtained the entire bounty for his time with Hancock's Veteran Regiment and had attempted to collect it in 1881. He was told that since he did not complete his full year of service, he got what he was due: $76.76. Sometimes it does not pay to be impatient.

A virtually penniless Lydia died on October 20, 1927, at the age of eighty-eight. Her body was sent to Oswego and interred in the Adriance plot.

The sad events in the lives of William and Lydia Adriance following the war demonstrate clearly how the privations William endured affected the rest of their lives. Had he not been forced to face the elements for extended periods, he probably would have been better able to provide for his family. Moving from Oswego, where he had spent much of his life, to an alien environment and an uncertain future was surely an act of desperation on his part. And Lydia, like many widows of the period with numerous children and few resources, scrabbled as best she could for the rest of her life to support them and herself. Her tenacity demands admiration.

Chapter 2

Francis M. Pease

How long I may survive only God knows.

Francis M. Pease's ancestral roots are shrouded in the mists of time. Members of this family came to the New World in the seventeenth century, and two of them, John and Robert, were among the founding settlers of Enfield, Connecticut. Several genealogists, including Frederick S. Pease in 1849 and Reverend David Pease in 1869, made herculean attempts to chronicle the history of the descendants of the earliest members of the family but were unable to complete their task since letters went unanswered and incomplete information hindered their research.

Francis's grandfather, David Pease, born in Enfield on March 2, 1785, married Elizabeth Archer, born on April 24, 1785, in Williamsburg, Virginia. Elizabeth's antecedents are as mysterious as her husband's. The Archer family was prominent in Virginia, but I was unable to locate an Elizabeth born in 1785. The couple's marriage date is unknown but is estimated at about 1815. The only document that can be definitely assigned to them is the 1850 census, in which David and Elizabeth Pease, both sixty-five, were enumerated in Northeast Township, Erie County, Pennsylvania. Elizabeth's birthplace was erroneously given as Connecticut.

David and Elizabeth's tombstone in the North Scriba Cemetery records that he died in Rome, New York, on August 9, 1853, and that she died on September 18, 1863, almost certainly in Scriba, because Francis Pease, the

According to their epitaph, Francis Pease's grandparents were born in Connecticut and Virginia. *Author's collection.*

subject of this chapter, mentioned her in a letter he wrote shortly after the Battle of Gettysburg: "The last letter from home was dated June 14. It reached me seven days later. I was sorry indeed to learn that mother's [Christiana] and grandmother's [Elizabeth] health is poor."[92]

Clearly, the Pease family moved around. Albert, Francis's father, was born in Camden, Oneida County, New York, on March 3, 1816. The 1820 census for Rome, New York, shows David Pease, twenty-six to forty-four, and a female aged twenty-six to forty-four. Both were thirty-five years old at the time. The family contained two male children under ten, one of whom I guess to be Albert, Francis's father.

Francis Pease's maternal antecedents are just as obscure as his paternal line. According to her tombstone, Christiana G. Worden was born in Remsen, New York, on October 25, 1812—but who were her parents? *The History of Remsen* mentions a Revolutionary War veteran, John H. Worden, who came to Remsen after first settling in Herkimer County. He reportedly married Rebecca Clyde, but this account is untrue. The author telescoped the lives of two men, causing endless confusion for researchers. George Horace David Worden (1838–1905), a great-great-great-grandson of John H. Worden, reported that his ancestor died in Stephentown, New York, sometime prior to the spring of 1794, when the "Widow Worden" (that is, Sarah Brayton Worden, circa 1748–circa 1817) moved four of her five sons—John Lanother (1772–1848?), Joseph Warren (1773–1852), Isaac (1777–1856) and Edmund (1779–1863)—to Trentontown, Oneida County.[93] John Lanother is the important son for the Pease family. He married Rebecca Clyde, and they were the parents of Isaac (1804–1877), Joseph (1805–ante 1870), John L. (1806–post 1892), James (?–1871) and Stephen (1809–1886). *The History of Remsen* states that John and "Aunt Becky" resided in the Remsen area "for many years."[94] Christiana was probably their daughter because theirs was the only Worden family known to be living in the Remsen area when she was born in 1812. It is possible that her birth was considered insignificant beside the births of five brothers. It is equally probable that her birth was simply not reported to any compiler.

According to George Horace David Worden, John L., William, Edmund and Isaac eventually moved to Prospect, New York. John may have died in 1848 since he does not appear on the 1850 census. Aunt Becky was enumerated in both the 1850 and 1860 censuses as living in Remsen. In the later census, she was listed as residing with Isaac. Rebecca's birth and death dates greatly interested her descendants. In the 1850 census, she gave her age as 78, but by 1860, she had suddenly become 98. One source states that she died in 1862 at the age of 102, while another states that she died in Prospect in 1868 at the age of 106.[95]

Albert and Christiana perhaps married circa 1842 since their first known child, Jane, was born in 1843. She died in 1847 and was buried in the North Scriba Union Cemetery. Her birthplace has not been established, but the 1865 state census reveals that the couple's four living children were born in Oswego County. Since Albert does not appear individually on any census before 1850, he probably lived with his parents until he married Christiana, moved to Oswego County and settled in Scriba.

By 1850, Albert and Christiana were the parents of four more children: Francis, or Frank, as he was commonly known, 1844; Elizabeth Artemisia, 1849; Emma Jane, 1854; and George F., 1857. Before examining Frank's life, let us look at these siblings.

Elizabeth Artemisia, or Lizzie, was a teacher. She married a widower, Herbert Sterling Morehouse (1847–1914) in 1875. By 1893, they were living in Rulo, Nebraska. A letter she wrote to the editor of the local newspaper clearly described the ecological, sociological and political conditions existing in southeastern Nebraska:

Albert and Christiana's tombstone offers proof that Christiana was born a Worden and lived in Remsen, New York. *Author's collection.*

Perhaps a meager description of this part of the country may not be amiss to many of [your] *readers in my native county. This is the southeastern county of Nebraska, joining Brown County, Kansas, on the south. In climate, soil and production, it would be hard to excel. The rapid advancement in educational interests in these two counties is said to be second to none. The political outlook is rather dubious here, many democrats affirming that the present administration had done nothing it agreed to, and that they will not vote for that party again; the soldiers' rights to pensions being denied to so many is too bitter for many of them to swallow.*

Mrs. L.A. Morehouse[96]

Lizzie bore two sons, Albert George (1884–1957) and Francis E. (1888–1967). Morehouse died on April 4, 1914, and Lizzie on April 1, 1924. Their death certificates show that both were buried in Rulo.

Emma Jane, Frank's other sister, married John Everleigh in 1887. According to the 1900 census for New Haven, they were the parents of an adopted daughter, Mabel Vivian (1898–1988). Emma died in North Syracuse on November 1, 1926, and was buried in the North Scriba Union Cemetery.[97]

Vivian Everleigh graduated from Syracuse University at the end of the fall semester in 1920 and announced her "engagement" to Kenneth Ray LaVoy (1897–1980), a World War I veteran. Ostensibly, they were to be married on January 29, 1921.[98] In reality, the couple had been married in Rochester, New York, on October 25, 1919. They gave the identical address—1025 Goodman Street North—but whereas LaVoy said he was a student, Vivian lied and said she was "at home." Somehow, they managed to keep their union secret.[99] A short notice announced that the couple would marry on Saturday, January 29, 1921.[100]

The youngest Pease child was George, and census records reveal he was a cook. The 1930 census, however, reported that he was an inmate of the Craig colony in Groveland, Livingston County, founded in 1896 for epileptics. George died there on June 8, 1933, at the age of seventy-nine. His obituary read: "He was devoted to his friends and relatives in this vicinity and known for his kindly nature."[101] George never married. He was buried in the North Scriba Union Cemetery.

Let us now return to Frank, who was born February 28, 1844, probably in Scriba. His military record described him as five feet, eight inches tall with a light complexion, brown hair and blue eyes. Frank, like his father, was a cooper. Somewhere along the line, he acquired the rudiments of an education. Thanks to him, we have an eye-witness account of events occurring on the first day of the Battle of Gettysburg. He also kept a diary that has disappeared. The last known owner was Mabel Pease Hart, Frank's daughter. When she died, perhaps it passed to her son Duane Hart (1908–1980), but where the diary is now is anyone's guess. If it no longer exists, it is a great loss for local history. Fortunately, Charles McCool Snyder had access to it when he was writing his history of the 147th Regiment, and he quoted freely from it.

Frank, age eighteen, enlisted when President Lincoln called for a three-year draft of 300,000 men in August 1862. The incentives were tempting: the state and county bounties amounted to $130. Recruits were also promised $150 from the federal government at war's end. Perhaps equally important was the disgrace attached to a draft. This sentiment is clearly expressed in the following: "Some people are deceiving themselves in regard to a draft. They argue that because the time is extended, no draft will be made. We tell them that they are deceiving themselves. Men the Governments wants [*sic*], and men it will have. Unless our quota is raised, drafting will take place in this county. Let no man say after he is drafted that he did not have fair warning."[102]

On August 25, 1862, Colonel Andrew S. Warner received permission to raise a regiment, ultimately designated the 147th New York Infantry Volunteers, and on August 30, Frank enlisted in New Haven. He was officially mustered into Company F as a private on September 22. Company F was composed of recruits from Mexico, Palermo and New Haven.[103] The entire regiment, composed of 837 enlisted men, departed Oswego on September 27, 1862. As events unfolded, the 147th Regiment became famous for its participation in many battles. If only for Gettysburg, a battle the Confederates "were supposed" to win, the 147th would have been hailed for gallantry and bravery in the face of overwhelming odds.

We have Elmina Spencer, a famous Civil War nurse, to thank for information concerning the early movements of the 147th Regiment. According to her, the regiment boarded a train on September 27, 1862, bound for Washington, D.C. The soldiers arrived at Geneva at 2:00 a.m. on September 28 and then boarded steamers. They disembarked about 9:00 p.m., marched a quarter of a mile and then boarded a train for Elmira. The train broke down near a place called Havana. After receiving needed repairs, it proceeded to Elmira, arriving about noon. Here the men rested

Elmina Spencer was revered by the Oswego County veterans, who lobbied successfully to obtain her a pension. *Author's collection.*

until ordered back on the train at 4:00 p.m. They crossed the Pennsylvania border near sunset.[104] Elmina's last published article told how the regiment bivouacked at Camp Chase, near Washington, D.C.[105]

The regiment's next destination was Tenallytown: "On the 6th inst. Mr. [R.S.] Kelsey made a visit to the camp of the 147th Regiment at Washington. The regiment was then under marching orders for a village called Tenallytown, about three or four miles from Georgetown, Maryland. The men are described as being in the very best of spirits, though somewhat fatigued from their journey."[106] Conditions at Tenallytown were horrible. The 147th was put to work building forts and rifle pits to protect the nation's capital. After two months, the troops were ravaged by malaria, dysentery, typhoid, jaundice and desertion.[107] Morale flagged as building projects "consumed more time than drill, and the men were soon grumbling."[108]

Life in the army was not entirely dull. Private Pease noted in his diary that when an unexploded cannonball fell into the camp, several soldiers went looking for it, hefting and measuring it. Then, to tease the pickets, they dragged it about until boredom overcame them.[109]

At the end of November 1862, the 147th was transferred to the Army of the Potomac. Stationed at Falmouth, Virginia, the regiment witnessed the bloody Battle of Fredericksburg on December 13–15. Their duties involved policing, guarding railways and receiving and forwarding supplies—hardly the assignments for which they had enlisted. Christmas was difficult, particularly because of the awful food, which consisted of hardtack, coffee, pork, soup and raw onions. Frank wrote in his diary, "I thought of Santa Claus and the Christmas presents which were dealt out on the day; thought to myself I would like to be home to enjoy Christmas, but I am in a different business, and must attend to it."[110]

The 147th was transferred in the first week of January 1863, along with the rest of the brigade, to the First Army Corps, and conditions changed: "General Paul, an old army officer, directly set himself to the task to perfect the organization and discipline of his brigade, attending to the details of drill, sanitary policing, and the personal and soldierly bearing of officers and men."[111] In the meantime, General Burnside was being pressured to find another opportunity to defeat Lee, who had trounced him at Fredericksburg. Burnside's plan was good: he would move his forces across the Rappahannock River and encircle Lee's army, camped outside Fredericksburg.

The weather, however, became a worse enemy than the Confederates. Although January had been fairly dry, Burnside waited too long to act. A nor'easter brought rain on the evening of January 20, and it continued throughout the following day. Wrote Adjutant Dudley Farling of the 147th Regiment:

> *Our brigade and regiment started at noon on Tuesday past. The weather was fine and the roads in fair condition at that time. After proceeding some ten miles, however, and night closed upon us, the rain began to fall fast and steady and continued all night. In the morning, we moved on, but the roads had broken up. The artillery and supply trains got stuck in the mud. We marched on till 4 P.M. through a perfect mortar bed and in the rain, when our brigade and in fact the whole army was compelled to halt.* [On Friday morning], *the order came for the great army to retrace its steps, as it was impracticable to proceed any further, as the wagons and the artillery could not proceed, and it is impossible for an army to move without supplies of food for soldiers and ammunition and big guns. We started back and marched fifteen miles through indescribable mud, through fields and forest, leaving hundreds of dead horses and mules behind which expired from mere exhaustion.* [We] *came up on Saturday afternoon and took our old camp, which was most disgustingly muddy and dirty, as an Ohio regiment had occupied it during our absence.*[112]

This was the first real soldiering experience the 147th encountered, and it gave the troops a taste of what lay ahead. As an aside, on January 26, Burnside was relieved of command, and General Joseph Hooker was appointed in his place.

Having learned that winter campaigning was expensive and foolhardy, the Army of the Potomac did little until April, when the weather cleared and the mud dried, making marching and transport easier. At this time, the 147th Regiment was attached to the Second Brigade, First Division, First Corps. On April 28, the soldiers broke camp at Bell Plain and headed for the Rappahannock. The strategy was to lay down pontoon bridges, cross the river and head for Chancellorsville. We do not have Frank Pease's description of the four-day fight, but Joseph Dempsey wrote that once the pontoons were laid, the 147th was the first to cross. Fierce fighting ensued for the next several days, and the 147th was in the thick of it, holding the center against repeated Confederate attacks: "The rebels charged seven times on Sunday and were repulsed every time by our centre, which was our weakest point. We then marched to Chancellorsville, reaching that place [on May 2] about six a.m. We formed the second line of battle—the regulars the first—we being the reserve to them. Our boys were very anxious to have the rebels give us battle here, as we had very strong breast-works."[113] Despite desperate fighting, the Union forces were eventually forced to retreat. Dempsey records that the 147th Regiment recrossed the pontoons last.

The men, Dempsey says, thought they were going to Fredericksburg and were disappointed when they realized they were heading for Pine Grove, near Falmouth. Here they recuperated from the typhoid, fatigue and diarrhea acquired during the campaign.[114]

The bravery of the 147th did not escape notice of superiors. Brigadier General Lysander Cutler, commander of the Second Brigade, reported, "The several regiments of this brigade behaved with great coolness during the time they were under fire from the enemy's batteries—on April 29 and 30 and May 1 and 2—and were at all times ready and eager to be led into action. The 147th New York Volunteers were under fire for the first time and behaved with the coolness of veterans."[115]

Chancellorsville provided a prelude to Gettysburg. Fresh from his latest victory and recognizing that Virginia's resources were exhausted, General Lee decided to attack Union forces in their own territory, perhaps even capturing Washington, D.C., and forcing President Lincoln to sue for peace. The Army of the Potomac was again in turmoil. General Hooker lost the confidence of his subordinate officers and resigned in a huff. On June 28,

George Meade took his place, and he ordered his officers to impress upon the troops the significance of the Confederate presence on Union land: "The enemy is now on our soil. The whole country looks anxiously to this army to deliver it from the presence of the foe, [and] our failure to do so will leave us no such welcome as the swelling of millions of hearts with pride and joy, as our success would give to every soldier of the army. Homes, firesides and domestic altars are involved."[116]

We are fortunate that Frank Pease sent a letter to his family describing the Battle of Gettysburg. He reveals that his regiment marched from Falmouth, Virginia, through Maryland and into Pennsylvania, arriving on June 30. He wrote:

> *The rebels are over in the direction of Gettysburg, six or seven miles from here.* [On] *July 1st we were routed out at daylight and ordered to march. We started at seven o'clock. When we got within a couple miles of Gettysburg, we saw two or three shells burst in the air. There was hard fighting to be done, and we were ordered to load, which we did without delay. Then came the order, double quick, and the men started towards the front on a run.*[117]

Fierce fighting ensued, and Pease found himself surrounded by Confederate forces in the famous railroad cut. The 147th had not received the order to retreat until it was too late for many of the soldiers to escape. Pease wrote:

> *Finally we got the order to retreat, and we lost no time in obeying, leaving an awful sight of dead and wounded upon the field. As we retreated, we got into a railroad cut or ravine. We were moving as fast as we could, which was not very fast because the ravine was crowded and there were a good many wounded men that had to be helped along. After we got into the cut, the rebel bullets whistled over our heads. Soon the Johnnies were upon both sides of us, standing upon the banks in large numbers, and we were compelled to throw down our arms and surrender.*[118]

By 10:00 a.m., Pease was a prisoner of war. His captors handed him over to Union officials, and on July 5, he set out for parole camp at Westchester. He had to refrain from fighting until an exchange of prisoners could be arranged with Confederate officials. Nevertheless, he concluded his letter home on an optimistic note: "We have good news from the front. Lee has been routed, and it is believed that he will be unable to cross the Potomac, as it is very high and the bridges have been destroyed. Best love to all you and give my respects to the neighbors and the boys in the shop. Tell them that I have been in one big fight and helped whip the rebs."[119]

At the conclusion of the three-day battle, only 79 of the original 380 men who entered the battle on July 1 answered the roll. Back home, the newspapers kept citizens apprised of the wounded, dead and missing. Among the names of those in Camp Parole was that of Frank Pease.[120] Not until August 7, 1863, was he released.[121] His muster roll records that he rejoined his regiment on August 15. On October 1, he was promoted to corporal. One month later, on November 1, he became a sergeant.

The 147th Regiment's last major engagement in 1863 occurred at the Battle of Mine Run in Virginia. General Meade was looking for a way to lead his eighty thousand union soldiers against Lee's fifty thousand men encamped in fortified areas south of the Rapidan River. He decided to cross the river and surprise the enemy. Because of heavy rains, however, Meade was forced to order a forty-eight-hour delay. Therefore, the crossing originally planned for November 24 took place on November 26. Muddy roads made transport of baggage and artillery difficult. While the Union troops slogged through the mud toward Robertson's Tavern, Lee moved his army east, hoping to cut off Meade's forces.

Fighting began on November 27 and continued throughout the day as both sides awaited reinforcements. First Corps, of which the 147th was a part, arrived late in the day after the skirmishing had ended. As Crisfield Johnson points out:

> *The remainder of the day and till about ten a.m. on the 29th was occupied in getting into position. The First Corps formed into line of battle and charged through the dense thickets and over ravines, preserving a perfect line when possible; when any part of the line was interrupted by some impediment, formed into columns by regiments, deploying into line again when the impediment was passed, preserving intact an unbroken and even front, and a continuous line of battle, until the enemy was driven across Mine Run. No maneuver could have been more perfectly executed on an even parade-ground. It was a beautiful sight.*[122]

The campaign ended abruptly because Lee learned of Meade's plans and moved some of his men, thereby depriving the Union general of any chance of success. Rations and fodder were in short supply. Roads were almost

The 147th Regiment's participation in the Battle of Gettysburg is commemorated by this statue. *Courtesy Darlene Woolson.*

impassable.[123] Perhaps most significantly, the terrible weather conditions enervated the Union forces almost beyond an ability to fight:

> *In the meantime, the weather had become intensely cold; the men on the skirmish- and picket-lines suffered terribly; some of the wounded were frozen to the ground. In the night, it fell to the lot of the One Hundred and Forty-Seventh Regiment, under Lieutenant-Colonel Harney, to picket the front across the run. No fires were allowed; they were in close proximity to the enemy, and the least noise would draw upon them a shower of bullets. When he withdrew the line, many of the men were so benumbed with cold that it was with difficulty that they could be urged to withdraw. The enemy had already made a movement to cut them off, and the regiment barely got across the run in time to escape capture.*[124]

While we have no record of Francis Pease's memory of the Battle of Mine Run, we are fortunate to have that of his commander, Lieutenant Colonel Harney, who wrote a letter to the editor of the *Oswego Commercial Times* that was published on December 26, 1863. He recalled that he and his troops broke camp early on November 26, crossing the Rappahannock and marching all day through heavily wooded land. At about 10:00 p.m., the men halted for a few hours' rest and were on the road again at 3:00 a.m. the following day. Having crossed the Rapidan, the Union forces were accosted by a band of Virginia guerillas who tricked some of the teamsters into taking the wrong road:

> *A large portion of the train followed until at last one of the teamsters, suspecting something wrong, refused to go any farther. A fight ensued, in which the teamster was killed; the guerrillas came out of their hiding places—some formed in line to protect others who employed themselves in robbing the wagons. They did not have much time to do their work, for three regiments of the first Brigade of our Division immediately deployed and, with a yell, charged on the rebels and sent them flying in all directions. Our boys ran them out of sight in less than five minutes.*

On November 28, Harney's men moved into position near the enemy at Robinson's Tavern:

> *Our regiment was detached, and I was directed to relieve a regiment of the Second Corps, which I did and had my skirmish line established before*

> *daylight. The enemy did not advance as was expected. Our Brigade was formed in two lines of battle (our regiment in the front line) and advanced through a thick growth of timber, driving the enemy before us. We then came to an open plain close to Mine Run and under the enemy's guns; we then halted,* [and] *the rain began falling heavily; companies I and G skirmished with the enemy until dark, we remaining in position ready to support them. At dark, firing ceased.* [On] *Nov. 29th and 30th the regiment remained under arms.* [On] *December 1st the regiment was detailed on picket duty. I was directed to cross Mine Run* [and] *hold and protect two bridges which had been thrown across the creek during the day. I crossed and posted the men close to the rebels, and ready for a fight next morning, but it was decided not to make an attack on the rebel works, so I was ordered to fall back and destroy the bridges, which I did at 8 o'clock the next morning, taking up the bridges and setting fire to the timbers, without losing a man. The night was piercing cold; I got chilled through and have not got over it yet. We found it would not do to attack the rebels—the reasons of this you have learned through the papers some time ago. The regiment did very well during the expedition; only a few of the conscripts were badly frightened. But if this regiment is properly handled this winter, it will be a good one in the spring.*[125]

Harney had written his letter on December 17 while in camp at Kelley's Ford, where First Corps was bivouacking. He described the wretched conditions in Virginia:

> *Our camp is situated on the south side of the Rappahannock and close to Kelley's Ford. You must almost know the place, you have heard so much about it in the newspapers. It is a desolate looking place now. Kelleysville is almost torn down; the few houses that are left standing are well marked with shot and shell which passed through them. The hills in the vicinity of the Ford are also well marked with field works, rifle-pits, &c. The country around is dotted with the graves of the brave men of both armies who died gallantly fighting for the cause each loved best. Our Division Camp is situated in a large belt of timber. The men have their huts all finished; some of them are very nice and comfortable, but the location is unpleasant and unhealthy; the camp now looks like a vast bed of black mortar. The surface is covered with a thick coat of decayed vegetation—men and horses traveling through the camp will sink, the horses up to their knees in some places, and the men above their shoes. There are quite a*

> *number getting sick already; indeed it would almost make a man sick to look at the camp this morning.*[126]

A type of typhomalaria laid many soldiers low, especially affecting the newer soldiers.[127]

First Corps finally went into winter quarters near Culpepper, Virginia, where the land and the water were more advantageous for recovery.[128]

In May 1864, another battle important for the destiny of Francis Pease occurred. After months of drilling and preparing, the 147th Regiment found itself transferred to the Fifth Corps, Fourth Division, Second Brigade. By this time, General Ulysses Grant had taken charge of the Army of the Potomac. He planned to cut up Lee's forces as badly as possible while heading to and occupying Richmond. Lee, on the other hand, was determined to save the city.

Troops of the Fifth Corps crossed the Rapidan at Germanna on May 4, hoping to entice Lee's forces out of hiding and fight south of the Wilderness. The plan failed because two of Lee's corps encountered three of Grant's moving south, and all-out fighting began on May 5. A short description of this area reveals why Grant wished to avoid it:

> *The area of the Wilderness consisted mainly of underbrush and brackish water, 70 miles wide and 30 miles long. Fighting in this place became an ordeal. Both sides were often invisible and were only able to move by the use of a compass and the sounds of the gunfire from either side. Also, much of the brush in the area caught on fire, and so many of the wounded died or suffocated due to the fire. With the smoke-filled woods caused by underbrush fire, many troops lost their way and ended up shooting at their own.*[129]

By the time the battle ended on May 6, the 147th had sustained 171 casualties, including 55 missing.[130] Of these, Francis Pease was one, and this time, his luck ran out. The prisoner exchange program was no longer being observed. One reason was that General Grant decided that sending Confederate soldiers back to the South simply meant the Rebel ranks would be replenished. An equally significant objection concerned black Union troops. Once captured, the Confederates refused to include them in exchanges, contending that they were slaves, not soldiers.[131] By the time Pease was captured at the Battle of the Wilderness, POW camps had sprung up in both the North and the South.

In his quest for a pension, Pease alleged that he spent time in Danville Prison, Andersonville and Florence Prison. The Memorandum from Prisoner of War Records supports his assertion, and several of Pease's wartime comrades also confirmed his allegation. While we do not know for certain how Pease traversed from one prison to the next, we do have the recollections of Reverend Isaac M. Foster, a corporal in Company H, Forty-sixth New York Infantry, who was also captured during the Battle of the Wilderness. Foster never tired of telling his tale and traveled to many places to lecture on his days as a prisoner in Confederate prisons.

At one gathering, Reverend Foster said he found two friends among the captives:

> *1,500 of us were taken to the Orange Court House, twenty miles distant. There we were packed in box cars, ninety-five men in a car, to be taken to Richmond. But the plan was changed, as our cavalry had been interfering with communication to Richmond, and we were taken to Lynchburg. We were crowded so thickly in the cars that in order to get down, the row in the rear of the car would have to get down and take the row ahead between their knees. Everybody had to sit at once. We had to get down together and get up together. Arriving at Lynchburg, we were taken out into the country a couple of miles, where camp was made.*[132]

Foster recounted that he stayed at the camp only a few days before being transferred to Danville, where the prison buildings were old tobacco warehouses numbered one through six, each containing several stories and holding up to seven thousand prisoners. Number 1 was reserved for officers and Number 6 for black troops. Rations included black bread, corn bread, coffee, small amounts of beef, soup, cabbage and rice. Later, rations were decreased to the point where each man received only one and a half pounds of bread per day.

According to Major Abner Small of the Sixteenth Maine Volunteer Regiment, also a prisoner at Danville: "Our quarters were so crowded that none of us had more space to himself than he actually occupied, usually a strip of the bare hard floor, about six feet by two. We lay in long rows, two rows of men with their heads to the side walls and two with their heads together along the center of the room, leaving narrow aisles between the rows of feet."[133] His description was supported by Foster, who said that 1, 500 men were packed so tightly into one of the rooms that they scarcely could turn around. Food, said Foster facetiously, was "one bean to about six soups…and meat was the liveliest that one ever saw. It would walk away without difficulty at all. Out of the dead came the living."[134]

After a short stay at Danville, Foster (and perhaps Francis Pease) was transferred to Andersonville: "Here 45,000 prisoners were packed into a space that seemed insufficient to hold the 15, 000 that were there when we first arrived."[135] Andersonville, or more correctly, Camp Sumter, was situated on a railroad line in inland Georgia. The Confederates thought that this territory, so far untouched by the war, could provide protection for guards and adequate supplies for the captives. Much has been written about this place, from both Union and Confederate viewpoints. A cursory Google investigation into books written about Andersonville is mind-boggling. Add to it contemporary newspaper editorials and articles, magazine pieces and soldier memoirs. Careful examination of many early publications reveals exaggeration, propaganda and outright lies, but the truth is that thirteen thousand men perished at Andersonville and hundreds returned home so ill that they either died shortly thereafter or, as in the case of Francis Pease, suffered severely throughout what little time was left to them.

The Memorandum from Prisoner of War Records contains no evidence to prove that Frank was confined to Andersonville. Other documents, however, attest to his incarceration in the South; for example, a report dated October 25, 1881, and another dated June 9, 1882, each state that Pease was paroled in February 1865 and reported to Camp Parole on March 12. Two members of the 147th Regiment later testified that they, while also imprisoned there, saw Pease. Charles Dashner (1836–1907), a private in Company A, had been captured on October 19, 1863. He spent time in another infamous prison, Belle Isle, before being transferred to Andersonville in March 1864. Belle Isle was a low-lying island on the James River near Richmond, Virginia. Historian Mark Weber notes that at Belle Isle, "less than half of the 6,000 prisoners could seek shelter in tents; most slept on the ground without clothing or blankets. Many had no pants, shirts or shoes and went without fuel or soap. At least ten men died a day in vermin-ridden conditions of inexpressible filthiness."[136]

Dashner was transferred to Andersonville and recalled he was "there when said Pease came." He recalled that shortly after Frank arrived, he contracted scurvy: "[He] complained of being very sick and poorly, and he remained sick all the time I knew him in the said prison."[137] After both men returned to Oswego County, Dashner said Pease "told me that he never got rid of the pain in his breast."[138] Pease was referring to a condition called "chronic gastritis," which he mentioned throughout his pension application papers.

Pease's second witness was Oscar Merivale Coon (1846–1898). Coon was a member of Company C, 147th Regiment, and like Pease, he was taken prisoner the first day of the Battle of the Wilderness: "We were confined in the Rebel Prison at Andersonville, Ga.; that said Pease suffered with disease of the stomach while he was confined in said Rebel Prison and complained a great deal of suffering from said disease; and that said Pease suffered with disease of his stomach after being in said prison a short time [and] all the rest of the time of his confinement in said prison." Coon remembered that when he first saw Frank after the war he continued "to suffer from said disease continually to the present time."[139] Coon later wrote, "As we were acquainted from boyhood, we ate & slept together while in prison [and] was in close confinement in Danville, Va. then to Andersonville Ga. then to Florence, S.C."[140]

Byron C. Earl (1838–1907) and William Henry Rose (1844–1924) also offered supporting testimony. Earl had been a member of Company F, 147th Regiment, from August 1862 until January 1863. Rose was a private in Company G, 24th Cavalry. The men knew Pease from boyhood and worked with him as a cooper. They said that "when [Pease] came home on furlough from southern prisons in spring of 1865, he was very poor, feeble and emasiated [*sic*] but at expiration of his furlough returned to his Regiment, the 147 N.Y. Vols."[141] Thomas E. Farr (1832–1899) provided more evidentiary testimony. Farr was mustered into the 147th as a corporal. He confirmed that he and Pease entered the Battle of the Wilderness on May 5 and that Pease was taken prisoner. Farr added that Pease returned after nearly a year in Rebel prisons sick and unable to work.[142]

The most telling statement, however, came from Pease himself. In an undated document relating to his application for a pension, he pleaded, "I saw hard service with my Regt. as the records will show besides the many trials & hardships of a ten months' southern prison life eating cob meal & suffering in many ways beyond description."

Even allowing for the exaggerated and bitter memories of former prisoners, descriptions agree in one important point: the place was a death trap. Originally conceived of as a place where captives could be cared for more adequately than in Virginia, Andersonville suffered directly from General Sherman's scorched-earth policy. The unsanitary state of the water contributed significantly to illness among the prisoners. The stream running through the center of the camp was downwind of the guards' barracks and the cookhouse. John Stibbs, a member of the Twelfth Iowa Regiment and a prisoner at Andersonville, later recounted, "For a time, this creek was the only source from which our men obtained water; but in time, the creek bed and fully an acre or more of land bordering it became a putrid mass of corruption, into which the men waded knee-deep to secure water from the running stream."[143]

Prisoners and the guards were supposed to eat the same types of food. Records show that each man was to receive one-third of a pound of beef or pork per day and one and a quarter pounds of cornmeal. Sometimes the men were issued onions, peas, beans, molasses and even small amounts of salt. However, since rations delivered on any particular day were based on the previous day's roll, they did not take into account the increasing numbers of prisoners arriving in the meantime. To ensure all got something, the Confederates were often forced to issue short rations, a decision guaranteed to enrage their captives.[144]

Pease called eating "cob meal" the cause of his chronic gastritis, and Roberts's description of it is graphic:

> *The cornmeal fed to the prisoners was "unbolted," meaning that the bran and the kernel were not separated. Simply put, the cob was ground up with the corn. The unbolted cornmeal was largely indigestible, and it produced all types of intestinal disorders, the most common of which was diarrhea. To men already weak from hunger, the rough cornmeal acted like tiny razor blades in their lower intestines. Many Andersonville survivors claimed that they still suffered from intestinal distress decades after being released from the prison.*[145]

Dysentery, diarrhea, scurvy, lice and gangrene were rampant among the prisoners, and it was said that soldiers entering the hospital never came out alive.

After a sweltering summer, the Confederates encountered another problem. General Sherman was approaching, and the Rebels worried they would be compelled to defend Andersonville with ill-equipped, inadequate forces. They decided to ship the captives to other prisons, one of which was to be at Florence, South Carolina, and began the exodus in mid-September before the stockade was completely built. From diaries, we can reconstruct the timeline of transfers. Charles Hopkins, for example, departed Andersonville on September 11 and reached "the prison pen" at Florence shortly thereafter. George Crosby, a private in the First Vermont Cavalry, recorded that he left Andersonville on September 12 and arrived in Florence on the fourteenth. Francis Pease's transfer to Florence had to be during this same period.

Later in life, former prisoners of Florence Prison said conditions there were worse than those experienced at Andersonville because the men arrived already weakened from exposure and disease. Samuel Eliot of Company A, Seventh Pennsylvania Reserves, offered the following:

> *While at Andersonville, I did not suppose the rebels had a worse prison in the South, but I have now found out that they have. This den is ten times worse than that at Andersonville. Our rations are smaller and of poorer quality, wood more scarce, lice plentier, shelters worn out, and cold weather coming on. I have stood my prison life wonderfully, but now I am commencing to feel it more sensibly and am getting too weak to move about. To add to my misery, I have the scurvy in the gums.*[146]

John McElroy of Company L, Sixteenth Illinois Cavalry, whose memoir is considered exaggerated, reported that all the trees and brush were cleared at Florence very early and that those fortunate to get there first claimed what wood was available to make huts. All others were left to their own devices:

> *Those who had less eked out their materials in various ways. Most frequently, all that a squad of three or four could get would be a few slender poles and some brush. They would dig a hole in the ground two feet deep and large enough for all of them to lie in. Then, putting up a stick at each end and laying a ridge pole across, they would adjust the rest of their material so as to form sloping sides capable of supporting earth enough to make a water-tight roof. The great majority were not well off as these and had absolutely nothing of which to build. They had recourse to the clay of the swamp, from which they fashioned rude sun-dried bricks, and made adobe houses, shaped like a beehive, which lasted very well until a hard rain came, when they dissolved into red mire about the bodies of their miserable inmates.*[147]

Smallpox and yellow fever soon ravaged the prison. McElroy included insanity in his list of maladies afflicting the men, along with respiratory problems and gangrene.[148] Comparing rations of Andersonville and Florence, McElroy wrote, "Wretched as the rusty bacon and coarse, maggot-filled bread at Andersonville was, it would still go much farther towards supporting life than the handful of saltless meal at Florence."[149]

By November, the prison contained 11,424 prisoners, and plans were made for paroles and exchanges of the sickest.[150] Pease, however, was not paroled until February 1865. His prisoner-of-war record states that he was exchanged at North East Ferry, North Carolina, although it appears no such place formally existed. Michael Hill of the North Carolina Office of Archives and History has suggested that Pease was paroled in Pender County, situated in the upper reaches of the Cape Fear River. Wilmington, North Carolina, fell to the Union on February 22, and arrangements were immediately made for prisoner exchanges to occur between February 26 and March 4, 1865. Pease's parole on February 27 fits perfectly into this time frame.

How Pease got to Camp Parole, Maryland, is unknown, but his war record states that he arrived on March 12. It is possible, because of the length of time between release and arrival, that he was transported by sea. He may also have spent a few days at a field hospital before being shipped out. The next available date is March 17, 1865, when his thirty-day furlough was granted. The furlough was a convenient and inexpensive method for the government to use to rehabilitate thousands of former prisoners. Frank's time in Oswego is confirmed by copies of two train tickets, one from Oswego to Syracuse and the other from Syracuse to Annapolis, both dated April 17. He arrived on April 19. William H. Rose wrote, "In the spring of '65, we were both home on furlough. Saw him several times at his father's. He then complained of pain in stomach. We returned as far as Philadelphia together. He still complained of pain in the stomach."[151]

Upon returning to his regiment, Pease was deemed unfit for active duty and was sent to Camp Distribution, Alexandria County, Virginia, on May 7. This place acted as a headquarters for the U.S. Sanitary Commission, which provided hospital care, clothing and money for soldiers. On June 7, the 147th Regiment was honorably discharged at Washington, D.C., and the soldiers, including Francis Pease, made their way back to Oswego.

The folks at home were preparing to welcome them in grand style. Having heard that "the 'bold soldier boys' would prefer an entertainment of domestic cookery, served up by the hands of Oswego ladies, to all other receptions," the women divided into committees to solicit food: "If the ladies of the city undertake the work, it is needless to say that the veterans will have a reception which will rejoice their hearts."[152]

Frank returned home and swiftly fell ill. He wrote, "I was treated for several months soon after I returned home by one Dr. James Austin for stomach ailment, what the diferent [*sic*] physicians called Chronic Gastritis of the stomach."[153] He attempted to find work, as is evidenced by the following:

Since my discharge from the Army to the present time, I have resided at [Scriba] *and my occupation has been as far as follows as far as I have been able to perform manual labor: I have acted as an agent selling books, clothes bars, etc.; also have acted as agent in the fruit business in the season of such business in the fall of the year and some work in the small piece of land I now occupy, but all the harder part of the work on the said piece of land, such as plowing the ground & piling up stone, I have hired done, as I could not do it myself. I could not perform hard labor since my discharge from the army.*[154]

From information provided by Byron Earl, it appears that Pease, like many other former prisoners, was looking for subscribers for his own book on life in Confederate prisons, which he intended to write based on his war diary. For a time, he also attended business school classes in Oswego.[155]

Earl and Rose also recalled that Pease "was discharged [and] in short time came home in June 1865. He was soon taken sick and was sick for months with difficulty of the stomach and has been afflicted ever since...the doctors called his ailment Chronic Gastritis of the stomach. He is unfitted for performing hard labor and suffers very much with pain in his stomach, lasting at times for weeks insessantly [*sic*]. [We] know that aforesaid keeps a variety of medicine on hand that sometimes relieves him for short time."[156]

The following year, both Rose and Earl wrote letters to William Dudley, commissioner of pensions, detailing Pease's health problems after returning to Oswego County. Rose noted that in August 1865, he and Pease worked several days together in the cooper's shop: "He would have to stop work frequently, sometimes lying down with his stomach on a pile of shavings... said the pressure gave relief for a time." Rose went to Illinois in the fall of 1865, and when he returned the following year, Pease "looked haggard and worn. [He] said he was not able to work much. Don't think he was."[157]

Earl's letter also described Pease's condition in the years following his return from the war. Earl sometimes helped Albert harvest hay. He kept a log in which he recorded the dates he hired out, thus he was able to remember Frank's health at various times. For example, he noted that Albert rented the May Farm at Nine Mile Point in 1868 and that Frank was "living at home with his father & younger brother George." He continued:

By looking at my book, I find that I worked for Albert Pease...from July 28th 1868 to August 14th—14 days. Albert & myself would generally be in the lot by 7 a.m. Francis would not generally get out before 9 or 10.

> *He would not keep up with us and was awlways* [sic] *behind & and had to be helped out.* [I] *remember his complaining of not being well. Something was always the matter with his stomach. It was talked over in the family that Frank was not well. He had all the easy tinkering jobs to do puttering around the house.*[158]

Despite ill health, however, life could be good. Frank joined Beacon Light Lodge of the Independent Order of Odd Fellows, located in North Scriba. He was a member of the committee charged with writing a "resolution" upon the death of fellow member Robert J. Peck.[159] He took an interest in politics and represented Scriba at the first assembly district convention to choose delegates for the congressional convention.[160]

Probably Frank's greatest joy was Catherine, seventh child and fifth daughter of the Lords. Born in Oswego County on June 23, 1851, Kate had lived her entire life in the town of Scriba. On February 13, 1877, when Kate's sister Abbie and her husband, Otis Miner, celebrated their tenth anniversary, Kate and Frank tied the knot: "In connection with [the celebration], Mr. Frank M. Pease and Miss Kittie B. Lord were united in matrimony by Rev. Geo. D. Ellis, Mr. and Mrs. Miner acting as groomsman and bridesmaid."[161]

The 1880 Scriba census listed Kate and Frank as living there and gave his occupation as farmer. How much he was able to do on his own, however, is open to question. On March 5, he applied for an invalid pension, alleging he was qualified because he had contracted "Chronic Gastritis by reason of improper and insufficient food, being nearly starved to death while in Rebel Prisons—that he was taken a prisoner of war May 5th 1864 at Battle of Wilderness VA & was in rebel prisons at Danville VA, Andersonville GA & Florence SC." He claimed he was "nearly totally" disabled although he had attempted to make a living as a book agent and doing "a little light work."[162]

It is impossible to tell when or if Frank was examined in 1880, but Dr. George Johnson of Mexico, New York, examined him on September 14, 1881, and determined that he had a permanent disability: "Applicant has, of course, not any visable [*sic*] symptoms…only in his general looks which are bad…quite a good deal of epigastric tenderness and pain which is increased by active exercise or certain kinds of diet. He says that he vomits his food often." He also noted that his patient, who stood five feet, eight inches tall, weighed only 140 pounds.[163] Dr. Johnson's observation compares to that of Earl, who wrote, "I remember laughing at him or joking him about his stomach & belly being all sunk in. He was rather more that way than the generality of people."[164]

Pease consulted numerous physicians and took many medicines. Earl wrote, "I remember returning to my work at one particular time & hearing the family tell how Frank liked to have died. They sent for the Dr. & he finally got better."[165] Frank enlisted the services of Dr. Kilmer, "a traveling physician & Dr. G.D. McManus of Oswego NY." He also consulted Dr. H.L. Wilder, who testified that he was Frank's physician for nearly nine years. Wilder called his condition "progressive in its nature."[166] Two other doctors, Charles M. Coe and John Swinburne, were important for Frank's health. In 1882, Dr. Coe was working in Dr. Swinburne's medical office in Albany, New York. He traveled to Oswego in September and while there, Frank consulted him about his stomach ailment. Coe prescribed a diet and returned to Albany, later writing, "The following winter, I received a letter from [Pease] stating that his stomach trouble was growing worse and also that a tumor was rapidly growing below the right ear. I advised him to come to Albany for treatment. He came in March 1883." Dr. Coe again treated him for what he diagnosed as "irritative inflammatory dyspepsia of the most persistant [*sic*] kind." The plan was to develop a careful diet that would have a calming effect on the digestive system.

The tumor, however, was much more serious: "The tumor in the submaxillary and [parietal] regions also claimed attention, and from its rapid growth, it was thought best to remove it. It was excised Mar. 24 1883 by Dr. John Swinburne, assisted by Drs. Heath, Bowen and myself. He returned home in good spirits and soon after wrote a letter announcing continued improvement."[167] The remission was brief.

Before concluding the sad story of Francis Pease, let me divert briefly to his daughter Mabel Abbie, born on November 15, 1881. In her early adult life, she was a dressmaker: "Miss Mabel Pease has resumed dressmaking and will be pleased to see her old customers at her home, No. 106 East Sixth St."[168] Mabel's "honey" was Arthur DeForest Hart (1879–1964). Born in Lansing to Frederick and Sarah Jones Hart, Arthur became a mail carrier in 1904, rising through the ranks to postmaster at Oswego and retiring in 1948. He and Mabel were married on January 20, 1903, and had celebrated their sixty-first anniversary two days before his death on January 22, 1964.[169] Mabel died on July 7, 1965. She and Arthur are buried in Riverside Cemetery.

The Harts were the parents of one son, Duane (1907–1980), who became a professor at Clarkson University.[170] He married Clarice Jewell (1909–1988), who also died in Potsdam.[171] Their children were twins Joan Ann and Jean Arlene, born on August 23, 1930. Joan died on March 4, 2005, and Jean on

Mabel and Arthur Hart were married over sixty years. *Author's collection.*

Francis Pease's short life is honored with this handsome stone. *Author's collection.*

February 6, 2008, both in Massena, New York.[172] All are buried in Bayside Cemetery in Potsdam.

Kate Pease will appear again in a later chapter of this book, but it is now time to reveal the tragic ending of Sergeant Francis M. Pease of the glorious 147th. By 1885, Pease had succeeded in obtaining a pension, due in part, no doubt, to the efforts of friends who wrote letters to the U.S. Pension Commission. In March 1885, however, he was extremely ill: "Frank Pease is confined to the house. He went to New York some time ago to consult physicians in regard to an operation for the removal of a cancer and, on the advice of his physicians, returned home without submitting to the operation. He has now hopes of its cure by the use of medicine."[173]

Dr. Coe had moved to Lycoming in the spring of 1884 and saw Pease that summer. According to Coe, "There was a return of gastric trouble and enlargement of glands in the neighborhood of the old cicatrix. He refused all operative treatment and progressively grew worse in spite of all treatment directed to the stomach trouble. The tumor grew rapidly until it was as large as a two-quart pail. After a lingering illness during which he became greatly emaciated, he finally died on Mar. 11, 1886 from innutrition caused by diseased stomach together with extensive necrosis of the tumor."[174] Francis Pease was forty-two years and eleven days of age.

Would Francis Pease have enlisted in the Union army at the tender age of eighteen if he had been able to predict the awful consequences of his decision? Monetary incentives to serve had a great but not necessarily positive effect on families eking out a living as farmers. If there is an exemplar of the old adage "War is Hell," Francis M. Pease is it.

Chapter 3

Otis Mason Miner

A dangerous and precarious condition.

Otis Mason Miner was the direct descendant of a family that traced its origins to the time of King Edward III. As King Edward was passing through Somerset, England, in 1346 on his way to fight the king of France, Henry Bullman offered himself, along with one hundred of his miners and servants, as soldiers. For this gesture, Edward knighted Bullman as Sir Henry Miner.[175] His direct descendant, Thomas Miner, was born on April 23, 1608, at Chew Magna, Somerset. Thomas immigrated to the New World, where in 1633–34, he married Grace Palmer (1612–1690) at Charlestown, Massachusetts.

Thomas and Grace died only a few days apart in 1690 at Stonington, Connecticut. They produced thirteen children, beginning with John "The Captain" in 1635. Their progenies, male and female, followed the Biblical admonition, as they went forth, were fruitful and multiplied. A big problem associated with researching the Miner family is sorting out the family lines. For years, genealogists have confused the identities of women named Lydia Miner. One of these is Lydia M. Miner, daughter of Joshua and Martha Pierce Miner. I suspect the "M" was the initial letter of her mother's Christian name. Lydia M. was born in Massachusetts in 1800 and moved to Oswego County as a child. In 1864, she married a widower, Philo Burnham (1794–1878). Until that time, Lydia was unmarried, as confirmed by 1850 and 1860 Oswego City census records. In the 1870 census, however, she was listed as Mrs. Philo Burnham. She died on October 29, 1883, at the age of eighty-two, confirming she was born in November 1800. Her death date is corroborated by a legal notice appearing in the local newspaper in 1884 advising anyone with outstanding bills against her estate to come forward.

Lydia M. Miner Burnham is buried in the North Scriba Cemetery. *Author's collection.*

The second Lydia, whose middle name was Ann, was the daughter of Pierce and Emeline Ames Miner, meaning she was the niece of Lydia M. Miner. She was born in Scriba on May 6, 1833, and died on May 8, 1912.[176] In 1856, she married Philo H. Burnham, son of Philo Burnham and his first wife, Sarah Rice (1796–1862). He died on March 2, 1890. Philo H. Burnham and Lydia Ann Miner were the parents of six children: Hermon (1857–1862), Hattie (1859–1862), Flora (1863–1868), Martha Ruth (1866–1929) and twins Abbie May (1872–1952) and Alice (1872–1916).

Otis Miner would have no trouble tracing his lineage. He was a direct descendant of Thomas and Grace Palmer Miner, Ephraim (1642–1724) and Hannah Avery Miner (1644–1721), Ephraim (1668–1739) and Mary Stephens Miner (1672–1748), Rufus (1703–1760) and Mary Miner Miner (1705–1747), Joshua (1747–1776) and Rebecca Cottrell Miner (1744–1841), Joshua (1775–1854) and Martha Pierce Miner (1777–1864) and Pierce (1802–1895) and Emeline Ames Miner (1806–1865).

The family initially settled in Stonington, Connecticut. Joshua II and Martha were married in Massachusetts, and their first three children—Joshua III (1799–1834), Lydia M. (1800–1883) and Pierce—were born there. The family migrated to Oswego County in 1810 when Pierce was eight years old. Rufus (1804–1854) and Adeline (1806–1880) were born after the family moved. Pierce Miner married Emeline Ames on April 26, 1829. She was the daughter of Abner Ames/Eames (1765–1827) and Martha Burgess (1774–1823), both of whom hailed from Connecticut.

An ornate stone marks the graves of Philo H. and Lydia A. Miner Burnham. Many of their children are also buried in the family plot. *Author's collection.*

Pierce and Emeline were the parents of six children who survived to adulthood: Edwin Pierce (1830–1898), Lydia Ann (1833–1912), Joshua IV (1834–1908), Enoch (1836–1924), Willis "Willie" Henry (1841–1916) and Otis Mason (1843–1905). Two other children died young. The tombstone for Sarah Alida states that she died in September 1842 at the age of three years. Adeline's stone states that she died on October 13, 1847, at the age of nine years and six months. These children are buried in the Worden Sweet Cemetery in Scriba with their parents.

Otis was born in Scriba on July 19, 1843. As the youngest child, he might have been coddled by his parents and elder siblings, especially his sister Lydia. He acquired some measure of education and learned to read and write. Later in life, he became a cooper. When he was about to enter the Union army, he was described as being five feet, six inches tall with light brown hair and gray eyes.[177] Other descriptions listed his weight at about 150 pounds.[178]

When the Civil War began in April 1861, all parties concerned thought it would be of short duration, including President Lincoln, who had called for volunteers to serve a term of three months. The delusion was shattered on July 21, 1861, at Manassas, Virginia, in what became known as the First Battle of Bull Run. General Irvin McDowell, the Union army commander, and thirty-five thousand largely untested troops clashed with Confederate general P.G.T. Beauregard, leading twenty-one thousand rebels. The panic-stricken Union troops retreated in disarray to Washington, D.C., as the Rebels celebrated a significant victory.

Despite the Union's loss at the First Battle of Bull Run, some good did result. In addition to forcing both sides to realize they were engaged in a serious rebellion and to harden their resolve to fight, the outcome permitted the president to push through legislation to raise an army whose term of service would be two to three years. Oswego County had already raised the Twenty-fourth Regiment and now began recruiting for the Eighty-first New York Volunteers, which was known as the Second Oswego Regiment.

Recruitment started with a meeting at the Doolittle Hotel in Oswego on August 29. Otis, aged eighteen, and his brother Willis, aged twenty, enlisted on September 7, 1861, and were assigned to Company B when the regiment was formally organized on September 14.[179] Due to the slowness of filling the ranks, the troops did not leave Oswego until January 20, 1862:

> *Notwithstanding a blinding snow-storm, an immense crowd of people assembled at the Railroad Depot this morning to witness the departure of*

> *the Eighty-first regiment. All the men except a few in the hospital turned out, numbering about seven-hundred and fifty. They had a heavy march through the snow from Fort Ontario to the Depot but congratulated themselves on the fact that they are likely to be transported to a warmer climate very soon. The regiment will remain in Albany a few days to be filled up when it will be ordered southward.*[180]

The regiment did not actually leave New York State until March 5, 1862, when it was ordered to Washington, D.C., to defend the capital. On March 28, it moved to Virginia and became part of the Army of the Peninsula, assigned to Casey's Division.

The Eighty-first saw extensive action during Otis's and Willis's service, participating in twenty-one engagements and marching over six thousand miles of Virginia, North Carolina and South Carolina.[181] The regiment's initial action was at the Siege of Yorktown (April 5–May 4, 1862), when it did picket duty opposite Winn's Mill near the Warwick River and close to the Rebel forces. The regiment was sent to Northwest Landing, Virginia, where its responsibility involved breaking up smuggling efforts. The men also guarded the Dismal Swamp Canal. The Battle of Fair Oaks, however, would be of special significance for Otis, since he was wounded for the first time there. Also known as the Battle of Seven Pines, this conflict took place on May 31 and June 1, 1862. Overall command was in the hands of Union general George B. McClellan and Confederate general Joseph E. Johnston. The fighting was fierce, and the Eighty-first lost 137 killed, wounded or missing. The "inconclusive" outcome belied the heavy casualties suffered by both North and South.

A letter written by Lieutenant Hugh Anderson, a member of the Eighty-first, about his experiences during the fighting was printed in the June 10, 1862 edition of the *Commercial Times*:

> *There we were with a handful of men, as you might say, not 7,000 all told, and we kept our ground two hours, fighting and keeping back 30,000 rebels. Not until they had flanked us right and left and crushed us down in front did Casey's Division give way. We were cut to pieces—large numbers of officers killed and wounded. The Eighty-first had not been fighting five minutes before Col. DeForest was shot through the lungs, and Major McAmbley killed. The rebels attacked our Division first, it being the weakest in the army. We had been occupying the post of danger several days and were building a fort when attacked. The enemy advanced on*

us, regiment after regiment pouring down like rain. As their solid columns moved down on us, it was a fearful sight to see how our rifled cannon mowed them down. But they did not stop, knowing that they had superior numbers and hoping to crush us out with their large body of men.[182]

Captain David White also wrote home:

We have had a terrible fight. Our regiment's loss was considerable. My company was at the rear on every retreat. We several times fought from five to twenty minutes after the entire regiment besides us had fallen back. The enemy's force was probably not less than 40,000, while ours that engaged them was not more than 6,000. We had to fall back. The ground was strewn with dead. Our wounded were mostly carried off as we retreated. The rebels killed most of the others, and some of them in the most horrid manner.[183]

The same edition of the *Commercial Times* records the comment of Lieutenant John Oliver, who had been wounded at Fair Oaks and sent home. According to him, the Eighty-first Regiment "fought like tigers," and he fully corroborated the previous accounts received of the gallantry of the Oswego:

We have had a hard fight. The battle was hot, and the 81st was in its front for a long time, until we lost about two hundred and forty-six men killed and wounded. Our Company, when entering into the engagement, mustered fifty-eight men, and as it is the largest in the regiment, it is not probable that the 81st numbered more than 500 effective men in rank. Out of that number, we are short today, about 246. Before we retreated an inch, we had stood a crossfire from the enemy, who had flanked us upon the left, besides a terrible fire upon our front, until the batteries that supported and covered our right were taken by the rebels. Twenty men of Company B fell victims to the rebel shot, besides the instant death of our Major and the mortal wound of our Colonel. But each Company fought on its own hook and stirred not until it was surrounded on three sides. I don't know how any of us lived, for the balls flew like hail.[184]

Moore then lists the dead and wounded of Company B. Among the wounded was Otis Miner, who took a bullet through the right leg.

When Otis attempted to get a disability pension for his leg wound, he deposed, "After I was wounded, I was sent to the hospital at York Town

VA [and] stayed there until I was better. Then I was sent home."[185] The muster roll for May and June 1862 lists him as absent, although he was not wounded until May 31. Otis maintained that while his leg wound was treated at the York Town Hospital, he never received treatment for the foot cramps and rheumatism that first presented themselves on August 10, 1862.[186] He apparently returned to his post sometime in July or August since he was shown as present and owing the government for transportation from Albany to Baltimore.

Between 1862 and 1863, the Eighty-first Regiment saw active duty in many areas of the South, including Yorktown; Norfolk; Morehead City, North Carolina; and Bermuda Hundred. On March 23, 1863, Otis was promoted to corporal. At some point, Willis was also promoted.

In late 1863, the Eighty-first Regiment was stationed at Northwest Landing, Virginia, where Otis sustained his life-changing wound:

> *On the 27th day of November 1863 at North Landing, Va.,* [he] *was detailed on a foraging expedition with a detachment in command of Capt. John DeForest; that while standing at a rest with his hands clasped over the muzzle of his musket, a private in said detachment, to wit, Jeffers Boucher, accidently* [sic] *dropped his musket, which in falling struck the hammer of applicant's musket and caused it to discharge; that the ball passed through the right hand of the applicant, carrying away the third finger, permanently disabling the hand & also taking off the little finger of the left hand; that he is by occupation a clerk in a grocery; that from the time he left the service he has resided at Oswego, NY; that when he enlisted he was a cooper; that he is unable by reason of his injury aforesaid to work at his trade.*[187]

Strangely enough, Miner was not automatically discharged from service. Perhaps he did not want to leave his brother, or perhaps he was considered fit for duty, as he still possessed his trigger finger.

The spring of 1864 saw the regiment attached to the First Brigade, First Division, Eighteenth Army Corps, Army of the James. The men saw hard fighting in various parts of Virginia, including Bermuda Hundred and City Point. The fiercest battle, however, occurred at Cold Harbor between the dates of June 1 and June 12, with Friday, June 3, being the bloodiest. Forty-six years later, a reporter would write:

> *The Eighty-first New York Regiment...took a prominent part and with great loss. This battle was fought on June 3, 1864, and the memory of it*

> *is still fresh in the minds of those veterans of that regiment living. Every member of the color guard was killed. The regiment lost heavily in that engagement both in officers and men, eight of the ten captains being killed or wounded. The histories of the war show that in the battle of Cold Harbor, the Eighty-first New York lost more men per capita than any regiment in the corps which participated in the engagement.*[188]

As with so many other events pertaining to the Civil War, the weather played an important part in the planning. An eyewitness identified as "Ichthus," probably Captain Elias Fish of Company A, wrote: "The march from White House [Virginia] to Cold Harbor on May 31st and June 1st was a very severe one, the heat being intense and the roads exceedingly dusty, and many men fell out from their exhaustion, while some the truth compels me to say, skulked as the phrase goes in the army."[189] On June 1 and June 2, according to an eyewitness identified only as "An Officer," the Eighty-first was either kept in reserve or used to hold positions already taken by Union troops. Nevertheless, it lost sixty men. June 3 was to be much different:

> *At three o'clock on the morning of the 3d, we were again in line. The rain was falling furiously, and the men stood drenched and shivering and wondering what was to come next. The order was given, "Forward!" and we advanced in column doubled on the centre. We were to assault the next line of fortifications, which was more formidable than those we had captured, and as they hove in sight from the clearing beyond the woods, their long lines of muskets and artillery waiting to pour out their deadly volleys as soon as our columns should come within their range, was a prospect not at all inviting to those who were to participate in the conflict. The 81st had again been selected to lead the advance. The order was given to charge, and with a deafening yell, the 81st plunged in. The scene that followed baffles description and can only be imagined by those who have seen and heard the charge of a desperate battle-field. Two-thirds of the number fell in that charge. The regiment is very much decimated and is temporarily formed into three provisional companies. We are still in the front, however, and hope soon to bring up enough from our sick and wounded to be ready for heavy work again.*[190]

The Battle of Cold Harbor was on the minds and in the memories of soldiers and loved ones for years. Its anniversary was celebrated in many newspapers, including the *Oswego Daily Times*, which reported, "To-day was the forty-sixth anniversary of the battle of Cold Harbor, Va. in which the Eighty-first New York Regiment New York Volunteers recruited from Oswego County took a prominent part and with great loss."[191] Its fiftieth anniversary saw an even greater interest in the conflict. Noted one historian: "Fifty years ago today, the bloody battle of Cold Harbor was fought, in which Gen. Grant lost 10,000 men in 20 minutes. Seventy-five thousand men were hurled again and again against the Confederate works, only to be hurled back with fearful slaughter. Every effort to break the Confederate lines was useless, and the slaughter was terrible. Some called it butchery and a useless sacrifice of lives on the part of Grant."[192] Another article provided this insight: "The crowning horror was the fact that for two or three days, many of the dead and wounded lay uncared for upon the field because Grant and Lee were unable to agree upon the terms of a brief armistice. When at last an agreement was reached, the roll of the wounded had been greatly diminished and that of the dead correspondingly increased."[193] Grant himself acknowledged the foolishness of the battle: "Cold Harbor is, I think, the only battle I ever fought that I would not fight over again under the circumstances."[194]

When all was said and done, however, the troops and the officers paid for Grant's hubris. Union losses were estimated at more than 13,000, 1,705 of which were killed, another 9,042 wounded and 2,406 missing. Of the Eighty-first Regiment, 212 were killed or wounded and 3 missing. These figures constituted fully one half of the number of men from that unit engaged in the battle.[195]

If the soldiers of the Eighty-first were expecting a rest, they were mistaken. Grant abandoned Cold Harbor on June 12, and the regiment marched to Petersburg, where on June 15, it was instrumental in driving out the Confederates. In August, they were ordered to the Appomattox River and then to Bermuda Hundred. Engaged in the battle of Fort Harrison from September 28 to September 30, the Eighty-first was the first to plant its regimental flag on enemy ground. Here the regiment lost many more officers and soldiers during two days of fighting.

The Eighty-first Regiment regrouped and became a veteran corps, but without the services of Otis and Willis Miner. They were honorably discharged on September 13 at Bermuda Hundred and shortly thereafter returned to Oswego County. A local newspaper reported that Otis had with him a letter taken from a "secesh" at Petersburg, which was printed in full.[196]

Willis seems to have come through the fray unscathed. He was listed as participating in the Battles of Fair Oaks, Cold Harbor, Malvern Hill, Drury's

Bluff and others.[197] Under the terms of the Act of 1890, he applied for and received a pension.

As a disabled soldier, Otis was eligible to apply for a pension under the terms of the Act of July 14, 1862. The pension, if approved, would commence from the date of a man's discharge from service, provided he applied within one year. Should he apply later, it would start from the time of the application. Naturally, the government wanted to protect itself from those who were not disabled or those who falsified a disability. All sorts of forms were required, from the veteran's original claim to doctors' certifications to character witnesses and, if possible, letters from company surgeons and officers acquainted with the date and nature of the wound.

Otis Miner's pension file reads like a casebook for the Act of 1862. Alleging that his wartime wounds had rendered him incapable of pursuing his trade as a cooper, he applied for assistance with a sworn document dated November 21, 1864. He then appeared before Edward N. Rathbun, clerk of the Oswego County court, and related how he was wounded. He brought along two witnesses, James McLean and Arthur Buckingham, and named Robert H. Martin of Oswego as his legal adviser.[198]

The next step was a physical examination. This occurred on December 17, 1864, when Dr. C.C.P. Clark determined his disability was permanent and that he was two-thirds incapacitated from "obtaining his subsistence by manual labor."[199]As the result of the doctor's examination, Otis was to receive $5.33 per month beginning March 14, 1865, and retroactive to September 13, 1864. Over the years, Otis, like thousands of his fellow veterans, made application for pension increases. For example, in 1872, he petitioned for and was granted an increase to $8.00 per month following an examination by Dr. Macfarland, who ruled that he was totally disabled.[200]

The claims for pension increases provide vivid descriptions of Otis Miner's increasing invalidism. For example, in 1878, Dr. A.S. Coe noted that while "the use of the hand is not much impaired in warm weather, [Otis] is able to do but little in the fall and winter."[201] Appearing before Clerk of the Supreme Court John H. Oliphant on January 7, 1887, Otis made the following statement:

> *That he believes himself to be entitled to an increase of pension on account of his disabilities for which pension was granted him. That his hands have become much worse; that his right hand afflicts him severely; that his finger next to the index finger of his right hand has become useless and has become so lame and sore that it causes him much pain of*

> *his finger and in the joints of his right hand, and in consequence of the condition of his right hand, he is rendered wholly unable to procure his support by manual labor; and that he only has the use of his left hand to perform labor with and that his little finger of left hand was shot off. That in consequence of the condition of his hands, he deems himself entitled to an increase of his pension.*[202]

His request was received favorably, and on February 9, 1887, he saw his pension boosted to $10 per month. Petitions for subsequent increases fail to show that he was granted a larger monthly allowance.

It is unknown when or how the Lord and the Miner families became acquainted, but it is probable they knew each other through church and social events. The 1855 Scriba census lists Sarah Lord as a teacher, and perhaps Otis was one of her pupils. By 1865, she had been the wife of Otis's brother, Joshua, for five years. The 1870 Scriba census shows Otis and Abbie Lord Miner, Enoch and Zilpha (Root) Miner and Willis and Emily (Williams) Miner all residing on the same road as Reverend Lord and his wife, Laura. Pierce Miner, a widower, was living with Otis.

No matter how the two families became acquainted, the important point is that on February 13, 1867, Otis married Abbie Alzina Lord. They settled in Lycoming and produced two children: William "Bert" Birdsall, born on September 20, 1869, and daughter Katherine "Kittie," born on January 2, 1873.

Otis and Abbie became mainstays in local social circles. Otis was a member of Lewis P. Potter Post 573 of the Grand Army of the Republic (GAR) and in 1893 was elected junior vice commander.[203] In 1897, he became the senior vice commander.[204] Abbie was active in the Lycoming Methodist Protestant Church and was described as "a devout Christian."[205] She was also involved with the Ladies' Aid Society and in 1893 was elected treasurer.[206] The couple participated in Grange activities for many years. When Francis Pease died, Otis became his late brother-in-law's executor, and brother Joshua was named Mabel's legal guardian.

Despite the fact that Otis lost two fingers during the war, the 1870 census reveals that he was a farmer. Doubtless he was a diligent man, but he had very poor luck when it came to livestock. For example, one night, seven of his cows were killed by a train when they strayed beyond a downed BW&O Railroad fence. The railroad, it must be added, compensated him for his loss.[207] Equally unfortunate was an incident occurring several years later: "Otis Miner met with a painful accident yesterday while butchering. The hog, in some way, got one of his fingers in his mouth and bit it off. The doctor tells him he will not be able to do any work for several weeks."[208]

Like Otis, the eldest brother of the family, Edwin Pierce, must have been somewhat clumsy, since he lost his right hand while working at a sawmill. He also seems to have been a timid man, probably because he was unable to defend himself adequately. A newspaper article recorded how he was assaulted by a local bully, Byron Coon, who took great delight in constantly annoying Miner: "Coon attacked him, beating him shamefully and cruelly about the face and head."[209] The 1870 census records Edwin's wife was Ann, who died on January 30, 1876. Edwin died in 1898.[210]

Enoch Miner married Zilpha Root in 1862. They were the parents of three boys and two girls, one of whom, Hattie, died of typhoid fever on November 1, 1891.[211] Evidence suggests that the family moved to Kansas in late 1899 or early 1900. Enoch served as town assessor for many years. In 1899, the newspapers announced that candidates were needed to replace him and two others, and this fact may indicate when he moved his family out of the area. Enoch died on April 30, 1924, in Reserve, Kansas.[212]

Willis also moved west. His first wife was Emily Williams (1849–circa 1909). They were the parents of five children: Henry Jay (1869–1954), Frederick (1870–1953), George A. (1874–?), May G. (1878–circa 1880) and Mary Annetta (1891–?). May and Mary Annetta were born in Kansas. Emily died circa 1909, a date established by the census of 1910, which lists Annie E. as Willis's wife and shows that the couple had been married less than a year. Willis died in Salina, Kansas, on August 11, 1916.

Abbie saw her share of woe in those years. Her mother, Laura, died on March 28, 1888, with most of her children at her bedside. An obituary eulogized her: "She was married to Rev. Mr. Lord April 7, 1835, sharing cheerfully the labors of her husband in the Christian ministry until his retirement. After their long journey together, their paths now divide for a brief season."[213] Reverend Lord died in November 1895. His obituary read, "Mr. Lord was possessed of a clear intellect and a very logical mind. He was a sprightly, genial character and a universal favorite among his acquaintances."[214] Otis, too, began to say goodbye to parents and siblings. His mother, Emeline, died on December 3, 1865, having lived long enough to see her sons return from the war and to celebrate the end of the rebellion. Pierce Miner died on March 21, 1895.

Not all the events in Otis and Abbie's life were sad. In 1893, their son William married Grace Ure (1873–1927). Their son LeRoy (1894–1951) became an undertaker in Mexico. Bert was married twice. His second wife was Almira Larkin Yule (1878–1950), widow of John Yule (1850–1923). It appears that the couple wed circa 1930, as they appear on that year's census as husband and wife.

More happiness came to the Miner household on February 9, 1898, when daughter Kittie, a schoolteacher, married farmer Everett Mark Ames (1876–1964).[215] Kittie and Everett were second cousins through a shared set of great-grandparents, Abner Ames (1765–1827) and Martha Burgess (1774–1823). The couple lived in Richfield Springs and celebrated sixty wedding anniversaries. They became the parents of two sons, Otis I. (1901–1985) and Russell (1910–1990). Kittie died on August 10, 1958, and Everett on May 13, 1964. They are buried with his parents in the Twilight Rest Cemetery in Monticello, New York.

While contending with loss and sickness among his and Abbie's family members, Otis's own health steadily declined. He appealed to the Pension Board for more money and underwent a physical examination to determine eligibility. On September 26, 1900, Drs. James Stockwell, F.B. Foote and D.F. Acker reviewed the wounds to his hands and considered his complaints of "pain and lameness in shoulder joints, back & hips."[216] While they concurred he had a real disability in his hands, they declined to recommend additional benefits for his other allegations.

Otis suffered a stroke on May 31, 1903: "While at the church at North Scriba, Mr. Otis Miner of Lycoming, a veteran in the ranks of the G.A.R., was suddenly taken very ill. His head dropped forward, and those sitting beside him found that he was unconscious. It was said to be a shock, and it was thought he would improve in a few hours. An hour or two later, it was said that he had spoken and partially regained consciousness. This morning he is reported better."[217] While he recovered enough to talk, he remained bedridden and needing constant care. Another petition contained the following plea: "That my disability and complications has resulted in confinement to my bed since June 30th, 1903, and I request special examination at my house at Lycoming, NY. That since I last applied for an increase of my pension my disability has materially increased and specially so since my last examination by U.S. Pension Board."[218] Otis was so feeble that he had to sign his name with an "X." Dr. Henry L. Wilder, the family physician, attested to Otis's illness, describing his condition thus: "He [Dr. Wilder] desires to add that this claimant is entirely helpless and must be fed by another person and have constant watching and care by another person."[219]

Otis Miner clung to life until March 9, 1905, dying at his Lycoming home. An obituary said of him: "He was a farmer and had a wide acquaintance in the vicinity of his home."[220] Expressions of sympathy from the Grange and from the GAR were published shortly after his demise. The Bereavement Committee of the Grange issued the following:

> *Whereas Our Heavenly Father in His infinite wisdom has removed from this life our dear brother, Otis Miner, we bow in submission to the divine will of Him who doeth all things well; we still feel that a friend and brother has gone from our midst whose place will long remain unfilled...that the removal of such a life from among us leaves a vacancy and a shadow that will be deeply realized by all the members and friends of this organization and will prove a serious loss to the community and the public.*[221]

The Lewis Porter Post 573 of the GAR published a second bereavement notice, which read," We have lost a comrade tried and true, one who has ever dared to do his whole duty and by his acts and example lived up to the grand principles of fraternity, charity and loyalty. We tender his bereaved wife and children our most sincere and heartfelt sympathy."[222]

Otis and Abbie Miner were buried in the North Scriba Cemetery. *Author's collection.*

Otis was buried in the North Scriba Union Cemetery on March 13, 1905. He was a shining example of the proud stock that built this country. Descended from an English coal miner who loyally followed his king into battle, he, too, answered the call when his nation needed him. Later in life, he paid for his selflessness with constant, ever-increasing pain and illness. Despite his afflictions, he remained an upright, reputable citizen who loved his family and tried to provide for them.

Although Otis's worries were now over, Abbie's were only beginning. Because Otis died intestate, she was entitled to only a third of his estate. Fortunately, she owned her house and the lot on which it stood. Bert gave her a third of the profits from the sixteen-cow dairy. Abbie, sixty-one years old and with no one "legally obligated" to support her, quickly applied for a widow's pension under the Act of 1890. To prove need, various documents were filed. The farm was assessed for $3,250, with a cash value of $3,000. The house and lot had a valuation of $800. It was estimated that the house could be rented for $1 per week. Abbie's share in the dairy for 1905, the year Otis died, was approximated at $600, but with taxes, insurance and building upkeep, that figure was reduced to $450. In the end, the Pension Board granted her $8 per month. Only because Bert contributed to his mother's expenses was she able to carry on.

We shall meet Abbie again soon. For now, let us leave her and introduce Frederick Marvin.

Chapter 4

Frederick H. Marvin

Scion of Patriots

The subject of this sketch, Frederick H. Marvin, was a direct descendant of Matthew Marvin (1600–1678), who came to New England in 1635 and settled in Hartford, Connecticut, with his wife, Elizabeth (1603/4–1681), and four English-born children: Matthew (1626/7), Mary/Marie (circa 1629), Sara (circa 1632) and Hanna (1634). Three more were born in Hartford: Samuel (1647/8), Abigail (?) and Rachel (1649). Elizabeth's maiden name has been the subject of much controversy, and while some have proposed it is Gregory, no one can say what is for certain.

Matthew and Elizabeth's eldest son, Matthew (1626/7–1712), is best remembered for being one of the founders of Norwalk, Connecticut. His grandson, Matthew Marvin (1702–1745), married Elizabeth Clark (1711–1766) in 1730. They produced seven children, of whom the third, Ozias, is the most important for this study. In 1761, he married Sarah Lockwood (1745–1827). They were the parents of seven boys and five girls, of whom Ozias Jr. (1763–1848) was the eldest.

Many Marvin men performed military duty during the country's early years. Both Ozias Sr. and Ozias Jr. served in the Revolutionary War, chiefly in the defense of Connecticut. The elder Marvin achieved the rank of captain in December 1775 and next year saw action in New York State. He took part at Danbury Raid and was present at the New Haven Alarm on July 5, 1779. Ozias the younger served two terms of service, the latter under the command of his father. He was present at the burning of Norwalk, generally considered to be Connecticut's biggest battle, on July 11–12, 1779, when "a few American regulars and a lot of citizen soldiers, just regular people trying to protect their homes and families, fought…against overwhelming odds."[223] Nathaniel and William Marvin, sons of Ozias Marvin Jr. and Mary Bennett Marvin (1767–1815), saw action in the War of 1812. Nathaniel Marvin (1786–1868) moved from Oneida County to New Haven, Oswego County, in 1810. The previous year, he had married Julia Nichols (1788–1859) in Kirkland, Clinton, Oneida County. Johnson detailed Julia's harrowing trip to her new home, describing the Oswego frontier: "They came from Clinton, Oneida County, in 1810, transporting themselves and their scanty household effects in a flat or Durham boat by way of the Mohawk River, Wood Creek, Oneida Lake, and Oswego River to Oswego. Thence by lake to Pleasant Point. Mrs. Marvin ran the perilous passage of the rapids and falls of the Oswego River, near Fulton, in their frail boat." The couple settled on a farm commonly called the Tanner Place in the north part of the town of new Haven "when not a stick of the original forest had been cut."[224]

Nathaniel Marvin enlisted as a private in Colonel Jonathan Parkhurst's battalion, New York Militia, formed in 1813. Parkhurst had served in the Revolutionary War, allegedly as part of General George Washington's bodyguard. As a veteran, he was called upon to head a local militia in 1805.[225] Parkhurst migrated from Oneida County to Oswego County in 1798 and became supervisor of Mexico in 1801.[226] Not knowing the war had begun in 1812, he delivered a raft to Quebec, only to have it confiscated by the British. The story goes that he was so angry that he returned home and enlisted, forming the group called Parkhurst's Battalion. When the British assembled off the coast of the village of Oswego in early May, Colonel Mitchell ordered the militia to defend the fort and the supplies stored in Oswego. According to Churchill, in May 1814, "it was through his strategy that Oswego was saved. There being but 300 men at the fort and the British fleet approaching, he was ordered to prepare his men for battle. At his suggestion, the small army was marched out and around the hill appearing and re-appearing. The Britishers, thinking the woods were full of men, returned to Canada."[227] Parkhurst had a personal stake in the skirmish because when the British withdrew, they took all the supplies and equipment they could find, some of which was his.

Nathaniel Marvin undoubtedly participated in this battle and saw other action as well. As Simpson points out, "Since every able-bodied citizen was on call for militia duty in emergencies…it is fairly safe to assume that every

Nathaniel and Julia Nichols Marvin are buried in the New Haven Rural Cemetery. *Author's collection.*

man in this little community saw some service during the war, whether or not he was enrolled in Parkhurst's Battalion."[228]

William Marvin (1791–1857), Nathaniel's brother, is found on the 1814 list of landowners in Oswego County, but his War of 1812 involvement took place in Oneida County. Records show he was an ensign in Sylvester Gridley's Twentieth Regiment, New York Militia. Gridley (1769–1845), born in Connecticut, was living in Paris, Oneida County, when war broke out. He volunteered for duty and was appointed lieutenant colonel. Gridley's regiment saw action at Sackets Harbor in 1814, and although little is known about William's participation, he earned a veteran's pension that later devolved upon his wife, Catherine.

William Marvin was married twice, first to Polly Brayton (1797–1822), daughter of Caleb (1763–?) and Louisiana Bucklin Brayton (1766–?), on March 23, 1816. They were the parents of three children: Sarah Maria (1817–1839), William Waldo (1818–1891) and Harriet Newell (1822–1845). Only William Waldo lived to old age, reportedly dying in Sacramento, California. Polly died in New Haven, New York, on December 13, 1822, and was buried in the New Haven Rural Cemetery behind the Methodist Church. Her worn tombstone refers to her as "Polly, Comfort of Capt. William Marvin."

William Marvin is buried alongside his wives, Polly and Catherine. *Author's collection.*

On November 11, 1823, William married Catherine Prosser (1803–1883), the fifth child of Jonathan Prosser (1774–ante 1850) and Rebecca Hayes (1781–1855). William and Catherine produced four children: Eliza Ann (1825–1842), John Niles (1827–1858), George (1833–1854) and Frederick (1840–1924). William Marvin died on July 4, 1857, and was buried next to his wives and children.

Frederick H. Marvin was born on November 10, 1840, in New Haven. After his father died, E.S. Pardee of Fulton, New York, was appointed guardian while the will was probated.[229] Catherine never remarried. Her husband's War of 1812 pension, which she received until she died in 1883, was probably the primary reason for maintaining her widowhood. For many years, she made her home with Fred and his family.[230]

It is unknown how Fred and Sarah Jane Walker, who sometimes used her middle name instead of her first, became acquainted, but on August 24, 1862, the couple was married. Sarah Jane (1838–1908) was the daughter of John (1809–?) and Hannah Walker (1808–?). Born in Lancashire, she was the third of seven children.[231] The census for 1850 finds the couple and their six children—Mary, fourteen; James, thirteen; Sarah, twelve; Maria, ten; Fanny, seven; and Esther, one—living in New Hartford, Oneida County.

Another child, Delia, born in 1853, appears in the 1860 census for the same place. After 1860, John, Hannah, James, Fanny and Delia all disappear.

Frederick Marvin, a married man, would not be high on the draft list during the difficult year of 1863. In 1864, however, the situation changed. Thousands of three-year enlistments were ending, and the Union army was in dire need of soldiers, forcing the president to call for replacements:

> *Oswego County, again responding to the proclamation of the later-on martyred President Lincoln, calling for five hundred thousand additional troops to serve for one year, and which proclamation was dated July 18, 1864, set about the enlistment of another regiment to be added to the other Oswego County regiments that had already gone to war, and from which regiments of maimed and wounded men were continually returning home as leaves falling to the earth from trees smitten by the autumn frost.*[232]

It was considered shameful to be forced to hold a draft, and contemporary accounts warned that if sufficient enlistees were not recruited by September 5, one would be held immediately. A generous bounty was offered for one year of service: "On the one hand is presented a large bounty—the largest ever offered for soldiers—$700, together with the monthly pay of $16, making a pecuniary consideration of $892 aside from board and clothing for one year's service, and on the other hand a forced service, without any bounty. There can be no question which is the most desirable."[233] Fred and Sarah Jane Marvin probably depended on their farm for much of their livelihood. The bounty and soldier's pay undoubtedly looked good to them, especially since the end of the war was shortly anticipated. Marvin enlisted in Constantia, New York, on September 5 and was mustered into Company I of the 184th Regiment on September 16 with the rank of private. His muster papers described the twenty-three-year-old as being five feet, nine inches tall with blue eyes, brown hair and a fair complexion.

While Companies A, B, D and F left New York State on September 12 for their first deployment in Washington, D.C., Companies C, E, G, H, I and K remained in quarters until September 16, when they set out for Bermuda Hundred, Virginia. In December 1864, Company I was detached from the regiment and not reunited until after the Battle of Cedar Creek. Marvin and his fellow troops were sent to Fort Pocahontas, Virginia, a site that has only recently begun to receive detailed historical study. Located on Jamestown Island, Fort Pocahontas's story was long overshadowed by a better-known battle site, Wilson's Wharf, which lies nearby. Fort Pocahontas was constructed of high earthen walls designed to withstand enemy cannonballs. It was here on May 24, 1864, that Brigadier General Edward August Wild and two regiments of Union Colored Troops, numbering an estimated 1,600 men, plus a company of white cannoneers and two gunboats moored on the James River repulsed a Confederate attack led by Major General Fitzhugh Lee. The Confederate forces were approximately twice in number, yet the Colored Troops scored a decisive victory.[234]

Marvin spent several months on guard duty at Fort Pocahontas. He later blamed the time spent here for the onset of his health problems: "About the winter of 1864 & 5 while on duty with my company at or near Powahatan or Wilson's Landing Va. contracted fever, with chills & about the same time was affected with catarrh & was affected in my back in the region of the kidneys. Was also affected to some extent with my throat."[235] These ailments formed his claim for a pension when the Act of 1890 was passed.

On May 22, 1865, most of the 184th proceeded from Post Harrison's Landing to City Point, Virginia. A few days later, Company I arrived from Fort Pocahontas. They began mustering out on June 29, and the regiment set out the following day aboard the steamer *North Point*. The men of the 184th had seen service of less than a year but were welcomed home as conquering heroes. The 1890 Schedule of Veterans credited Marvin with eight months and twenty-five days of active duty.

The citizens of Oswego were preparing for the Fourth of July celebration and arranged to have the soldiers of the 184th brought from Syracuse to spend the holiday.[236] It appears that many did not return immediately to their bivouac, since on July 10, a notice was posted ordering the men to return no later than the following morning.[237] There was good reason to do so: when the men had been mustered out, not enough money had been available to pay them all.

Fred and Sarah Jane returned to farming and on April 24, 1869, welcomed their first daughter, Adah Belle. Carrie May followed on April 18, 1872.

According to the 1880 census, the Marvins were neighbors of the Lyman Legg family. Lyman and Nancy were the parents of Henrietta and William Buell Legg. On February 13, 1889, Adah and William Legg were wed. Their son, Harold Lyman, was born on January 9, 1890, and daughter Eva Mae came along on June 28, 1892.

The Leggs' marriage did not last. Their divorce was probably finalized in late November, because Adah, calling herself a widow, and Homer Coon, a former neighbor now residing in Rochester, crossed the Canadian border and were married on December 5, 1905.[238] Adah died only a few months after her father, on September 17, 1924, in Rochester.[239] She is buried in the New Haven Cemetery. Homer worked thirty-five years on Rochester's trolley system and died of a heart attack on March 8, 1944.[240] He is buried with Adah in the Marvin plot in the New Haven Cemetery.

Carrie's life was much different. On January 14, 1892, she married Orla Parkhurst (1867–1937), descendant of the same Jonathan Parkhurst who participated in the Battle of Oswego during the War of 1812. Parkhurst was a farmer, well known for his strawberries. The couple had one child, Mildred Irene (1896–1988), who married Charles Richardson (1895–1951). Orla died on January 20, 1937, following a massive stroke.[241] Carrie lived twenty more years, dying in the Syracuse Nursing Home on December 12, 1957.[242] Both she and Orla are buried in the Marvin plot.

Let us now return to Fred and Sarah. Through the years, they were involved in community affairs, Fred participating in the local GAR chapter, and Sarah taking an active role in the Women's Relief Corps. They knew Otis and Abbie Lord Miner well.

Fred's health gradually deteriorated, and when the Act of 1890 was passed, he applied for a pension. His application, dated January 16, 1891, stated he was "at times" wholly unfit for work because of "Rheumatism,

Carrie Parkhurst and Adah Coon were buried in their parents' plot. *Author's collection.*

Disease of Kidneys, Piles, Throat trouble & Deafness." Corroboration was provided by Dr. C.M. Coe, who examined the veteran and reported, "I have treated him at different times for piles, Lumbago, and an irritable condition of the bladder together with a condition of general debility associated with gastric catarrh. The piles and lumbago are especially severe at times, and one or the other often incapacitates him for manual labor for days at a time. There is partial deafness in both ears associated with catarrh."[243] Fred was granted a pension of eight dollars per month but apparently was unhappy with this amount, because on October 28, 1891, he was examined again, gaining little sympathy from the doctors. A year later, on December 21, 1892, three doctors examined him and concluded that he was eligible for a 4/18 disability for his catarrh and a 4/18 for "disease of rectum." They gave him no rating for his other ailments.

In 1893, Fred's pension was suspended. Eventually, he was informed that he would continue receiving payments, but at the reduced rate of six dollars.[244] If that decision was not insulting enough, a local conspiracy must have cut to the quick. Edwin J. Lawton was Fred's neighbor, Lycoming postmaster and notary public. Because he signed several depositions and applications, he knew about Fred's actions. Apparently enraged at what he perceived as an attempt to defraud the government, he complained to the commissioner of pensions: "[Marvin] enlisted in the 184 NY, was only a few months from home, received a bounty of one thousand dollars. He is now the owner of a large farm, a fine house, large and commodious out buildings…and capable of performing manual labor the year through and is in much better circumstances clear from all encumbrances than one person in twenty in the county on an average."[245] Lawton was incorrect about the bounty. Nevertheless, he, Alonzo Scott and D.L. Whaley protested Marvin's entitlement to a pension. Each appeared before special examiner S. Hotaling to testify against him. Lawton, while protesting his friendship with Marvin, said he purely wanted to see justice done: "Mr. Marvin is well off. He is a hard-working man, works hard every day in [*sic*] his farm and sometimes goes out to help his neighbors. I never knew him to be sick a day."[246] Scott took issue with Fred's claim that he was entitled to a pension because of deafness: "I have not discovered deafness." Like Lawton, Scott described Fred as "hard-working and industrious."[247] Lastly, D.L. Whaley testified that he, like Lawton and Scott, was acquainted with Marvin. He never knew him to be sick and noted that he was indeed most able to earn a living with his hands: "So far as I know, he is a sound man. I think him able to earn a support by his own manual labor."[248]

Hotaling recommended Marvin's pension be stopped as of May 31, 1894, but apparently the termination never occurred, because on June 5, 1894, D.W. Jones, medical examiner, reported to James R. Fritz, chief of the Board of Revision, that Fred's pension was justified and should be increased to the original amount of eight dollars. By the time Fred became an elderly man, however, the government had passed the Act of 1920, which effectively declared old age a disability. At the time of his death, he was receiving a pension of seventy-two dollars a month based on his need for "the regular aid and attendance of another person."[249]

The year 1908 brought bereavement to Fred. He and Sarah traveled to Rochester to visit Adah and Homer, and while there, Sarah died unexpectedly on September 28. Her obituary refers to her religious devotion: "Mr. and Mrs. Marvin were converted under the labors of the Rev. C.M. Boughton in 1875 and united with the Methodist Protestant Church of North Scriba charge, Onondaga conference. To this church they have given most earnest and faithful service."[250] In addition to her immediate family, she was survived by Mary Anne (wife of Henry K. Townsend), Maria (wife of John Quinn) and Esther (wife of Henry Fiske). Her body was brought back to Oswego County and buried in the New Haven Cemetery on October 2, 1908.

Fred soon found new happiness with Abbie Miner, whose self-perception was demonstrated by the fact that she gave "lady" as her occupation on their marriage license. The couple wed on October 25, 1909, with Bert Miner and Carrie Parkhurst as witnesses. They then set out for a short wedding trip to Rochester and Buffalo.[251]

Fred and Abbie lived harmoniously until his death in 1924. Over the years, his health spiraled downward, and in 1923, he became so weak that he was unable to get out of bed to care for himself. Adah wrote to the Pension Commission, begging for help: "Mr. F.H. Marvin is not able to attend to nature calls unaided. He is confined to the bed all the time and has to have constant care. He is not dressed, and has not been for some time. He was taken sick or confined to bed since July 14, 1923. I am his daughter and am caring for him continually. Age of myself, 54."[252] The gravity of Fred's illness is revealed in a letter written by Dr. Wilder: "Mr. Marvin's health has been failing for the past year. Together with other ailments he is suffering from Carcinoma [of the] right inguinal region, which has become an open sore. He is confined to the bed, at times delerious [*sic*] and needs the constant care of nurses both night and day."[253]

Dr. James Stockwell examined Fred on December 6 and elaborated on Dr. Wilder's description:

> *Alleges that last July a swelling developed in right inguinal region, attained large size and ruptured in four weeks, discharging profusely, offensively and continuously; intense pain that continues; required and still requires frequent, voluminous dressing. There is a large, freely discharging sinus just inside Poupart's ligament on the right side; have doubts of malignancy, but believe that an abscess from a suppurating appendix opened spontaneously at the point indicated. This claimant is so totally and permanently helpless from abscess and fistula, old age and heart disease that he requires the regular personal aid and attendance of another person.*[254]

Frederick H. Marvin died on January 2, 1924, and was buried next to Sarah on January 5.

Abbie's children had assisted her in obtaining a widow's pension when Otis died. She was probably horrified to learn that another woman was claiming to be Otis's widow and was therefore entitled to his pension. Margaret Elizabeth Capper (1849–1921) married a Canadian named John Minor (1843–1878) in 1867. Minor told his wife that he had served in the Civil War, but she had no tangible evidence that she deserved a widow's pension when John died in 1878, allegedly from the tuberculosis he claimed he had contracted while in the army. Margaret applied for assistance on several occasions, and the situation came to a head in 1918 when she deposed that John had traveled to New York City from Canada shortly before the war broke out when he was only seventeen years old. According to this version of the story, John met a cousin, Willis Miner, who urged him to enlist using the name of Otis M. Miner from Oswego. The almost-one-hundred-page file documenting Margaret's quest contains letters and depositions from friends, relatives and government officials who did their best to find John

The Marvin family stone pays tribute to Fred's military service. *Author's collection.*

Minor's outfit—under any name. While one pension commissioner described her story as fanciful, another said that when she came across the name of Otis M. Miner of Company B, Eighty-first New York Volunteers, while searching military records in Chicago, she jumped to the conclusion that John and Otis were identical. She accused Abbie of being Otis's sister whose real name was Lizzie and that Lizzie/Abbie and Otis were fraudulently receiving the pension Margaret claimed was hers. Newton Coe, postmaster of Lycoming, came to Abbie's defense, testifying that he had known her and Otis all their lives and that they indeed had been husband and wife. Although Abbie was the innocent party in this affair, she had to be upset and worried every time she received a letter from the government.

When Abbie married Fred Marvin, she relinquished the pension she was receiving as Otis Miner's widow. When Fred died, she was eighty years old, and her feebleness can be discerned from the way in which she signed her name on her declaration for a remarried widow's pension under Section 2 of the Act of September 8, 1916.[255] Thanks to the efforts of Kittie and Everett, Abbie's pension was restored at the rate of thirty dollars per month. She was receiving this amount when she died in Richfield Springs on May 24, 1926. Her body was returned to Lycoming, and the funeral was held in her old home. She was buried next to Otis in the North Scriba Union Cemetery. She left behind her son and daughter, three siblings, three grandchildren and three great-grandchildren.[256] An obituary eulogized her thus: "From a child, she had been a devout Christian and, like Dorcas, 'full of good works and almsdeeds which she did.'"[257]

Chapter 5

Himan P. Dutcher

You bet I am.

Himan P. Dutcher was a colorful character, possessing wit, charm and a definite interest in the ladies. The local newspapers were full of stories about his fishing exploits, his many wives and his reminiscences about the Civil War and the part he played in it. Of all the veterans whose stories appear in this book, Himan is the most fascinating. So great was his penchant for bending or stretching the truth that even now I am unsure that I can tell his story accurately. We have a pretty good description of the man. Documents consistently reported that he stood five feet, three and half inches tall. He had a fair complexion and blue eyes. As a young man, he had "light" hair, perhaps reddish-blonde.

The "mystery" of Himan Dutcher begins with his name, as it was variously spelled Himan, Heman, Hyman or Hiram. Although his tombstone clearly reads "Himan," he himself also used Hiram, as evidenced by a document he notarized on May 21, 1925. The muster-out roll of June 29, 1865, used the name Hiram. This interchange of names baffled bureaucrats in the U.S. Pension Department, one of whom tried to clarify the situation by writing, "Himan and Hiram Dutcher are identical." On another form, "Hiram" was crossed out and "Himan" substituted. Despite the fact that he was married multiple times, the only known extant letters are those written by his last wife, Gladys Ruth Griffiths, who generally referred to him as Himan. Accordingly, I have decided to use this name.

Himan's heritage is murky. He and his brother Gilbert first appeared on the Oswego, New York census roll in 1850 as children of Laurens and Laura (Bennett) Horton. Gilbert had been born in 1844 and Himan in 1846. The 1855 state census, however, gives their correct surname of Dutcher. In 1860, they were again assigned the surname of Horton. The question therefore becomes: who *was* their father?

The marriage license for Himan and his last wife records that the father of the groom was Peter C. Dutcher. Corroboration can be found in brother Gilbert's death certificate. Identifying Peter Dutcher has resulted in much confusion for genealogists, as it was a very popular family name. My choice for Himan and Gilbert's father is a man found solely in early military records whose name was Peter C. Dutcher, born circa 1815. He served twice in the U.S. Regular Army and for both enlistments gave his name using the middle initial C. Taking into account Peter's birth date and place of origin, Herkimer County, Simeon Dutcher Sr. and his third wife, Elizabeth Mott are good candidates to be his parents.

Himan once said that his father fought in the Indian Wars, and Peter C. Dutcher matches that description. He first enlisted in Company D of the Second Dragoons on August 19, 1837. He was just over five feet, six inches tall and had gray eyes, brown hair and a fair complexion. Dutcher was discharged as a corporal at Fort Shannon, East Florida, on August 19, 1840, at the expiration of his enlistment. While in Florida, he was part of the effort to pacify the Seminoles.[258]

Dutcher returned to New York State and married Laura Bennett, a native of Kingston, Ontario, Canada. In the 1855 census, Laura Bennett Horton said she had lived in Oswego for sixteen years, meaning she had come to the area in 1839, presumably with her parents, Augustus and Abigail Bennett. Dutcher and Laura married sometime between 1840 and 1843 when he reenlisted in the army.[259]

Peter C. Dutcher's military record states that he rejoined the army for a term of five years on October 26, 1843, in Buffalo, New York, where he was stationed at the Buffalo Barracks. Assigned to Company C., Second Regiment, he patrolled the Great Lakes, attempting to maintain the peace on the frontier.[260] This enlistment did not extend to its expiration in 1848, since on May 24, 1845, he deserted. He was apprehended on May 31, taken to Fort Ontario in Oswego and later transferred to Madison Barracks at Sackets Harbor for a court-martial. He was dishonorably discharged on October 25, 1845.[261]

Dutcher returned to Oswego, reunited with wife and son and in August 1846 became a father for the second time. After that, he disappears, dying sometime before 1849. Himan once said he had been born in the Shepherd Block on East Second Street. He also said he "grew up in a military atmosphere, living with his grandfather at old Fort Ontario from the time he was three to eight years old."[262] He obviously was embellishing the facts. If he had lived at Fort Ontario, as he said, the time frame would have been 1849 to 1854. Joshua Hibbard, Himan's step-grandfather, and his wife, Abigail, set up housekeeping in the Fourth Ward after his discharge in 1846. The 1850 census shows that Himan was living with Laura but also shows that Joshua and Abigail lived next door. Perhaps Himan spent a lot of time with his grandparents.

Laura's second husband, Laurens/Lawrence Horton, born in 1807, was the son of Deacon Ezra Horton and Olive May of Union, Connecticut. He was a goldsmith and watchmaker. Why he moved to the Oswego area is unknown, but the date can be approximated by the fact that he married Almira Coe of Scriba on June 11, 1834.[263] They were the parents of two children, Emily (1835–?) and William Henry (1840–1883). Almira died in 1842 at the age of thirty-two.

Horton and Laura Bennett Dutcher married between 1846 and 1849. Neither widows nor widowers wasted much time finding new mates. Because Almira, their first child, was born on March 3, 1850, the couple probably married in May or June 1849. The 1850 census states that Gilbert, Hyman [*sic*] and Almira were living with Laurens and Laura in Oswego City. The 1850 census showed Emily and William living with their maternal grandmother, Phebe Coe, in Scriba, New York. Emily, fifteen years old, was labeled "idiot." William was ten. It is likely that after Almira's death in 1842, Phebe took over the mothering duties for her grandchildren. Emily's disability may have been so severe that it was thought expedient to leave her in familiar surroundings after her father remarried. It is also possible that Laura, already caring for three children, did not want to be burdened with a mentally disabled teenager. This theory does not explain why William continued to live with his grandmother, but again, his stepmother may have objected to caring for another woman's child.[264] Laura died on July 5, 1867. Her grave has not been located, but it is possible that her body was removed from the cemetery now covered by Kingsford Park School on West Fifth Street and reburied in the "City Plot" in Riverside Cemetery.

Emily was living with Phebe in 1870, but her grandmother died the next year. What happened then can only be guessed. At that time, she was thirty-seven, and her widowed father was living with Myra and Leonora, who no

Almira Coe Horton's grave in the Worden-Sweet Cemetery is decorated with a beautiful stone. *Author's collection.*

doubt did not want a disabled sister residing in their home. Possibly the easiest solution was to place her in an institution.

The year 1857 was eventful for the people of Oswego, and later in life, Himan Dutcher would use one of those events to embellish his own experiences. Joshua Hibbard and Abigail Bennett were wed on October 9, 1845, at the fort. The following year, Hibbard retired from the military, and

Phebe and Albert Coe are buried next to their daughter, Almira Horton, in the Worden-Sweet Cemetery. *Author's collection.*

the couple moved to the city's Fourth Ward. In 1854, they settled in what was described as a "shack" on West Fifth Street Road in Scriba. It was here on "one hot day, August 24th, 1857" that he was killed.[265] A contemporary account reported:

> *There were seven wounds found on the body of the murdered man—five in the head and two in the body, either one of the latter being sufficient to cause almost instant death. One gash was found on the right side, five inches deep, penetrating through the ribs in the vicinity of the lungs; another on the left side to about the same depth, directly above the heart. The face was badly disfigured by glancing blows, tearing the flesh, and the nose was nearly severed from the face.*[266]

Hibbard, a neighbor, Richard Van Buren and Van Buren's fourteen-year-old grandson Robert Brower had set out for Oswego that morning to do some shopping. They stopped at several taverns and returned home in the afternoon. Toward evening, Dennis Sullivan, running from the local constabulary on account of a drunken brawl in which he took part the previous night, approached the Hibbards, asking them for water. Joshua invited him in and directed Abigail to get him some food. The men indulged in a few drinks and some animated conversation, complete with the host's demonstration of a sword exercise. Abigail excused herself to return some borrowed sugar. When she got home, she found her husband dying from wounds caused by the sword. She accused Sullivan of the attack. He was found nearby, taken into custody and brought before Justice Clark in Minetto. News accounts say that to protect his person, twelve men volunteered to escort him to the jail in Oswego. The sword was located in the bushes not far from where Sullivan had been apprehended. The crime made news for months.[267]

How much of this yarn is factual and how much is fictional is open to debate, but one thing is clear: in later years, Himan interjected himself into the tale on numerous occasions. One story claimed that he and his grandmother found Hibbard dying in the doorway of the home.[268] Another reported that Himan was the boy who went to town with Hibbard and Van Buren the day of the murder: "Hiram P. Dutcher, of the East Side, Mr. Hibbard's grandson, lived with him at that time and drove to Oswego City with him on the morning of the murder but remained in Oswego over night. Had he returned, the tragedy might not have happened, and yet it is possible that he, too, would have met a similar fate."[269] That these statements were fabrications is borne out by the testimony of the trial witnesses. None mentioned Himan's presence, nor was he called to testify—although since he was only eleven, he might not have been considered a competent witness. We do not even know for certain that he was living with his grandparents at the time. Abigail Hibbard gave no indication that the boy was residing with her and her husband. In fact, her entire testimony supports the idea that she and Joshua were alone that afternoon. It made clear that she "left no one but Sullivan and her husband in the house when she went to Mrs. Van Buren."[270] Nowhere did she state that Himan was present or that he accompanied her on her errand. Van Buren and Brower made no mention of Himan in their testimony. Furthermore, it is reasonable to think that witnesses called to the scene would have mentioned the boy's presence. My conclusion is that Himan simply took advantage of an opportunity to aggrandize himself.[271]

Himan outlived all the people involved in the case. His stepfather, Laurens, died in 1881. Abigail died in 1889, and Gilbert in 1898. Himan probably thought he could embellish the details without much concern that someone would challenge his version.

Above: Joshua Hibbard is buried in Fort Ontario's cemetery. His worn stone gives the date of his murder. *Author's collection.*

Right: Laurens Horton and daughter Leonora are buried in Riverside Cemetery. *Author's collection.*

Although Himan's military service was brief, he wore it like a medal for the rest of his life. The termination of three-year enlistments in 1864 meant that the Union army desperately needed fresh soldiers, and President Lincoln was forced to call for replacements. The war meetings held in Oswego County led not only to Himan's enlistment but also that of Gilbert Dutcher, who later recalled, "We were mustered in at Elmira N.Y., and I think we left there three or four days after that and went to Harpers Ferry. There were four companies out of the Regt: A, B, D & F. After reaching Harpers Ferry, we were detailed to guard a wagon train to relieve Gen Sheridan in the Shenandoah Valley."[272]

The four companies went first to Washington, D.C., arriving on September 16, 1864. The next day, they marched to Fort Corcoran on Arlington Heights, remaining for four days. On or about September 23, the troops were transported by railroad to Harper's Ferry, where they encamped on Bolivar Heights until September 27. From there, they marched throughout Virginia until October 3, 1864, when they started from Harrisonburg for Winchester. Changes of orders resulted in camping at Millwood on October 14. Early the next morning, the men set out for Cedar Creek, where General Jubal Early attacked the camp on October 19. Robinson recorded:

This battle of Cedar Creek was the first engagement in which the detachment participated, and wherein it received its baptism of fire. It can truthfully be said that it sustained its part well, and materially aided in the final triumphant repulse and defeat of the Confederates. It must be remembered that at the time of the engagement, scarcely a month had elapsed since the members of the detachment had been drawn from the peaceful avocations of home life, and had but little or no acquaintance with military drill, tactics, or discipline.[273]

Himan would later recall:

The rebels got into our lines in the early morning, and before we knew what was going on, the front lines were broken and began to fall back. We were in the last row, and behind us were the cavalry. We got the order to fall in and then to advance. Then came the order to lie down, and how we did hug the ground. Finally an order came to fire and fall back in order. We did as directed, but soon there was crowding, the line wavered and then we were in full retreat, with the cavalry leading the way. We had retreated about six miles and the thousands of men were scattered all directions when suddenly there was a shout that Sheridan was coming. I was in a field about a quarter of a mile from the turnpike. As Sheridan saw the groups of stragglers, he turned his horse from the road, jumped a low rail fence and came up to where we were standing. I was tying a handkerchief around the fingers of a Pennsylvania soldier when Sheridan come [sic] *up. He heard one of the boys call me "Dutch" and calling out, "Come along Dutch, help me to rally these men and we'll be sleeping on our old camp ground to-night." He was as good as his word. At eleven o'clock that night, we had regained our position, taken nine hundred prisoners*

Himan Dutcher had not reached his eighteenth birthday when he enlisted. He would later say that he weighed less than one hundred pounds at the time. *Courtesy of the Scriba Historical Society.*

> *and captured forty-two pieces of artillery. No tongue can tell and no pen describe the feeling that came over those retreating and vanquished soldiers who that day fought every inch of that battlefield twice. I remember how I felt when I saw Sheridan leading the way down the turnpike with the members of his staff...all doubt and fear vanished. The fact that Sheridan was with us was enough. No harm could come to the troops with Sheridan in our midst. I believe that I felt that he could almost turn aside the wrath of God so great was my confidence in the man that day. I can't describe it, but thousands of others must have felt as I did, for they rallied to a man, and the day was saved. In my judgment, that ride was the most stirring war incident ever chronicled in any country in any time.*[274]

After the Battle of Cedar Creek, the 184th headed to Fort Russell, remaining there until December 3, when they headed for Washington, D.C. They arrived in the capital on December 4 and that afternoon were loaded on the steamer *Charlotte Vanderbilt*, with a destination of City Point, Virginia, where they remained until they were mustered out in June.[275]

On June 29, 1865, Himan Dutcher was honorably discharged from the Union army. He had served the Union cause for ten months and seven days.[276] He headed home on July 1, arriving in Elmira on July 2:

> *July 3—The regiment took a train for Binghamton, arriving at 12. After a vexatious delay for want of transportation, the regiment left at 5 P.M. for Syracuse, and arrived at that place about 12 o'clock midnight. The regiment without delay marched to the fair ground south of Syracuse and encamped in due form.*
>
> *July 4—Daybreak revealed the fact that during the night, all the regiment save about one hundred men and one or two officers had decamped and had availed themselves of a train of cars that had been sent to Syracuse by friends in Oswego, in waiting to convey the regiment to Oswego and places along the line of the road, and which would enable the men to meet their friends and participate in the national holiday.*[277]

It is not known how Himan was greeted when he returned to his family, although his brother Gilbert was definitely not welcomed with open arms.[278] It is probable that Himan, too, received a cool reception, because by November, he was living in Chicago.

It is now time to introduce the first of Himan's five wives, Mary Lodema Cole (1847–?). Her parents were Seth Cole (circa 1810–circa 1898) and Jane

Rowbotham (1826–1901). Lodema had three siblings: Margaret, Seth and Myron Ambrose. How and where Himan and Denia, as she was sometimes called, met will probably never be known, but we do know that they were married in Chicago on November 14, 1865.[279] Theirs was evidently a stormy marriage, because in 1874, Denia sued for divorce. In her initial petition, it was noted that:

> *Hiram has been guilty of extreme cruelty towards the complainant* [Denia]*; that is to say that the said Hiram Dutcher on divers days and times since said marriage has beaten, struck, kicked, and choked her and refused to furnish her with necessary food and clothing. And particularly, on* [or] *about the middle of the month of July A.D. 1867, the said Hiram Dutcher struck the complainant a violent blow with his fist, knocking her down and otherwise greatly injuring her, and in the month of February A.D. 1872, he kicked her and struck her with his fist and has ever since said marriage abused her in the most cruel manner and used towards her the most abusive and opprobrious language rendering the complainant's condition intolerable and her life burdensome and thereby she was forced to withdraw from his house.* [He]*...has given himself up to adulterous practices and...has committed adultery with divers lewd women...during the summer of 1868, the said Hiram Dutcher was affected with a vile and loathsome venereal disease contracted by his adulterous habits and practices.*[280]

Denia filed a deposition on August 4, 1874, in which she stated:

> *That she is destitute of the means of supporting herself during the pendency of this suit and of carring* [sic] *on and prosecuting her original bill. That she is in delicate health, a large portion of time being confined to her room unable to do anything by which to make a living or to earn money. Hiram Dutcher is in good health and is employed as an express man, earning and receiving fair wages averaging two dollars and fifty cents per day, and that he has means amply sufficient to enable him to advance there out...such sums as may be necessary for the abovementioned purpose.*[281]

Himan denied all Denia's charges:

> *The allegations in Comp*[lainan]*t's Bill are untrue; that he never has been guilty of extreme and repeated cruelty to his wife; that he never deserted*

> *her; that he has never been guilty of adultery nor diseased her. On the contrary…that she voluntarily and without his fault abandoned his bed and board. That she has been guilty of adultery with other men since her marriage, and by said adulterous practices contracted a loathsome disease and imparted same to him. He further states that he has no means whatsoever. That he is driving a team as a day laborer and is earning only upon an average of $1.50 per day and ought not to support a wife who, without just cause, has abandoned him and incurred unnecessary expenses by this suit. That he is ready and anxious for a speedy trial.*[282]

On November 14 (the couple's wedding anniversary), the court agreed that Denia's claims "are substantially true as therein set forth and that the defendant has been guilty of extreme and repeated acts of cruelty towards the said complainant and that the defendant has been guilty of adultery since his said marriage with said complainant. Therefore, it is ordered adjudged and decreed by the court that the bonds of matrimony heretofore existing between the complainant and the defendant be and the same are hereby dissolved and that all and every the duty rights and claims accruing to either of the said parties by reason of said marriage shall henceforth cease and determine, and that the said parties be severally at liberty to marry again in like manner as if they had never been married." Himan, who had not shown up to defend his case, was ordered to pay all costs. What alimony Denia got, if any, is unknown. There is nothing in the divorce papers suggesting she and Himan had any children, but her use of the words "in delicate health" may have been euphemistic for pregnant. Later, Himan said he was the father of two children, the elder of whom was born in 1867.[283] I have been unable to find any evidence of the existence of either of these children.

Tracking Mary's post-divorce life was difficult, but a Mary Dutcher died in Cook County, Illinois, on March 25, 1916, allegedly at the age of seventy.

The newly remade bachelor did not long remain unmarried. On September 1, 1875, Himan and Mary Ann Decker were married in Chicago. Mary Decker's parents, James W. Decker (1808–1881) and Dinah Gray (1814–1874), were married on December 15, 1831, in Elizabethtown, Leeds, Canada West (Ontario). They were the parents of seven children, some born in Ontario and others in New York.

In 1870, Mary Decker was a housekeeper for Amy Nickelson's family in Oswego. Her obituary revealed the following about her time in the city: "Mrs. Mary Dutcher, whom death has called away, was formerly a resident of this city and spent her early years with many who will mourn her loss.

Some fourteen years ago, she bid goodbye to all whom she loved so dearly and went to Chicago where, after two or three years, she married Mr. Hiram Dutcher, also a former resident of this city."[284] What persuaded her to leave Oswego is unknown, but possibly she traveled with a family in need of a nurse or a maid.

A short-lived happiness invaded the Dutcher home in 1883 with the birth of Clara Laura, who was only three years old when she contracted tuberculous meningitis. After a brief illness, she died on June 15, 1886. Her parents buried her in Chicago's Oakwoods Cemetery. Clara's death foreshadowed Mary's by a mere six months. Her obituary noted, "Mr. Dutcher held a responsible office in the Chicago post office but on account of the health of his wife was compelled to resign."[285] The couple was back in Oswego by November, a date confirmed by an unusual newspaper article. According to the text, "a Mr. Dutcher from Chicago" had approached Fort Ontario authorities seeking permission to dig on the north side of the hospital to look for a large cache of gold buried there by the French when they evacuated the area long ago. The story mentioned that Mrs. Oliver (Ellen) Fairtile, Dutcher's aunt, and two diggers accompanied him on the day of the attempt. Despite a lengthy search, the would-be gold hunters located nothing. Upon inquiry, Mrs. Fairtile revealed that she had obtained her information about the buried treasure from her mother, Abigail Hibbard. Joshua Hibbard was said to have been present when the gold was buried, and Mrs. Fairtile alleged that she had a detailed description of the locale. Mrs. Fairtile also said that Mr. Dutcher planned to return in the spring to try again.[286]

Mary Dutcher died of tuberculosis on January 16, 1887. Her obituary noted, "Mrs. Dutcher had many friends in South West Oswego, also Fruit Valley, who will mourn her loss."[287] She lies in Rural-Union Cemetery in an unmarked grave.

Himan suffered another significant loss when his grandmother Hibbard died on June 23, 1889, at the age of eighty-six. She was buried in Rural Union Cemetery, taking with her what she knew about Joshua Hibbard's murder.

Himan's movements for the next few years have been difficult to track, but the Oswego City Directories for 1890–91 and 1892–93 list a Dr. Hiram P. Dutcher boarding at the Ringland House. It was surprising to learn that a man who signed his military papers with an "X" had suddenly acquired medical credentials.

Himan was soon to take another matrimonial plunge. Catherine "Katie" Lord Pease, whose husband, Francis, had died in 1886, moved to the city

Abigail Hibbard lies in the Fairtile plot with her daughter, Ellen, and husband, Oliver. *Author's collection.*

in 1887.[288] She became a member of Trinity Methodist Church on East Utica Street. By 1890, Katie and daughter Mabel were residing at 92 East Cayuga Street.

Joshua Miner ran a grocery store on Bridge Street and at one time employed Himan Dutcher. Perhaps through the good offices of Sarah and Joshua, the widower Dutcher met the widow Pease. Katie Pease, aged thirty-five in 1887, may not have been in any hurry to remarry since she and Mabel were enjoying military pensions. If she remarried, she would be required to renounce her portion. When the relationship between Katie and Himan became serious can only be conjectured by their wedding date: March 11, 1891.[289] Her reservations about the financial consequences of remarrying may have been allayed in November 1890, when Himan became the first veteran in Oswego County to be granted a disability pension.[290] At that time, he was still living in the Ringland House. The 1895–96 city directory records that the family had moved to a house at 145 East Second Street. By 1897–98, the family was living at 106 East Sixth Street, where they resided until Katie's death.[291]

After Himan's marriage to Katie, he dropped the title of doctor. From 1895 to 1898, he was a tender at Lock 17 on the Oswego Canal. He was a janitor for the Church of the Evangelists in 1899. Always one to make the most of his opportunities, he applied (unsuccessfully) for the position of harbormaster in 1900.[292]

Himan also became a member in Post O'Brien 65 of the GAR. He and brother Gilbert were appointed to committees in preparation for Memorial Day, and they volunteered to decorate the cemeteries.[293] Himan (now called Hiram quite regularly) served as the post's chaplain.[294] In 1893, he was elected senior vice commander of the post.[295] There were the inevitable funeral services for deceased comrades: "In Riverside Cemetery yesterday afternoon, the bodies of Daniel Burke and Gilbert Dutcher were laid at rest. The G.A.R. post attended Mr. Dutcher's funeral in a body."[296]

A diphtheria epidemic swept across New York in 1899. Oswego newspapers were full of accounts of households under quarantine. Schools were closed, and Sunday school classes were cancelled. Public health officials quarantined affected households, although Oswego doctors did not strictly enforce the ruling. This laxity infuriated Dr. James Stockwell, the city's health officer, and after venting his anger at the local medical establishment, he sought approval to appoint five special deputy inspectors to enforce the restrictions. For his services, each man was to receive two dollars per day. One of those deputies was Himan Dutcher.[297]

Gilbert Dutcher married Helen Forsyth, and they became the parents of two daughters and a son. *Author's collection.*

Himan lost his Katie on January 22, 1904, to arteriosclerosis. An obituary read, "For three years, she had been an invalid, and despite the fact that she suffered much, she bore her trials with true Christian fortitude."[298] Another noted, "During her residence in Oswego, Mrs. Dutcher made many friends who will learn with regret of her death."[299] Katie was buried in North Scriba Union Cemetery next to Francis.

As noted above, in November 1890, Himan Dutcher became the first Civil War veteran in Oswego County to obtain a pension under the Disability Act. His original claim, dated June 28, 1890, contains this statement: "He has hernia on left side in groin, which was contracted in the service in line of duty at the Battle of Cedar Creek Oct. 19th 1864. He has never made application for pension for said disability on account of being unable to procure sufficient proof of occurrance [*sic*]." Himan described himself as a laborer and considered himself three-fourths disabled for manual labor. His original pension consisted of ten dollars per month. On February 20, 1891, apparently attempting to wrest more money from the Pension Bureau, Himan applied to the surgeon general for a truss.

Convinced that ten dollars was a paltry sum, Himan wrote the following to Congressman Sereno Elisha Payne:

> *I am almost laid up entirely. I am drawing ten dollars per month for rupture and disease of rectum. My rectum has been ulcerated so many years it has left a large vacum* [sic] *and I am laid up. Now what I pray you to do for me is this. The* [illegible] *for rupture whitch* [sic] *went in effect last fall would give me the full amount* [of] *the new law, which is two more than I am getting.*

The letter's date is July 12, but the year is missing. Perhaps it was 1892, since it is known that Himan was still getting ten dollars a month that year. Additionally, he gave his address as 28 West Bridge Street, the location of the Ringland House. What result Payne's intervention caused is unknown, but notations on Pension Bureau forms reveal that he contacted that office at least twice on Himan's behalf.

Himan fought aggressively with the government over his pension. In 1893, he initiated a nonstop campaign for more money. A medical examination on July 12 determined that due to the hernia, he should be disabled at the rate of sixth-eighteenths. After receiving a letter from the Bureau of Pensions dated October 7, 1893, stating that he was not disabled from earning a living by manual labor, he retorted with the following: "I, Himan Dutcher,

Although Catherine was buried with Francis Pease, her stone gives her surname as Dutcher. *Author's collection.*

the claimant in Pension Claim No. 507619, would say that I am unable to earn a liveing [*sic*] and support my family by manual labor by reason of the following disabilitys [*sic*] to wit—left Hernia, disease of rectum, injury to right knee, rheumatism, kidney trouble."[300]

The doctors who examined Himan on November 29 concluded that his tumor was "easily reducible" and noted that he wore a truss. Although they refuted his claims of a rectal disease and kidney problems, they conceded that he "walks with a decided limp, favoring his right leg at the knee joint. We can find no objective signs to account for this." Himan told the doctors that he had received the injury by falling two years previously. To bolster his claim for an increased pension, Joshua Miner and his son Arthur offered their testimony: "That we are personaly [*sic*] acquainted with Himan Dutcher the applicant and that he is unable to perform manual labor to such an extent as to earn a living for himself and family."[301]

No record has been found to determine whether Himan got an increase, but perhaps he received nothing, since he petitioned again in February 1894. This time he based his claim not only on his hernia but also "piles," an affliction he had allegedly suffered for fifteen years. The doctors, led by Dr. Stockwell, concluded that Himan was entitled to a disability of 8/18ths for his hernia and 7/18ths for his hemorrhoids. When the Bureau of Pensions disallowed his petition in a letter dated April 3, 1894, Himan gathered his forces for another charge. Dr. J.S. Howard examined him on April 17 and reported the severity of the hernia, adding:

> *The prostate gland is tender, swollen and painful on pressure. He has to rise some 4 times at night and has to evacuate the bladder about once an hour during the day. The problem with the knee joint began and was caused by a fall striking on the right knee 2 ½ years ago and has continually troubled him since. He can walk with difficulty and can only bend the knee to a right angle. The said Himan Dutcher is suffering at the present time from permanent disabilities…these disabilities are inguinal hernia, enlarged prostate, and Chronic Synovitis of the right knee joint.*

Supporting evidence resulted from an examination performed by Dr. H.D.C. Phelps on April 21. Dr. Phelps reported inflamed testicles, chronic colitis, ulcerated rectum, shortness of breath and hand tremors. Like Dr. Howard, Dr. Phelps concluded that Himan was unable to do "hard manual labor or much of any at present and not able to earn a support for himself and family."

Himan now enlisted the aid of another friend, F.L. Smith, vice-president of the Oswego Hardware Company: "The writer has known Himan Dutcher for the past twenty (20) years, he having been in my employ some years ago. He is at present unable to perform any labor, being totally disabled."[302]

The records do not show what the Bureau of Pensions thought of the latest round of exams and references, but Himan must not have been pleased, as another physical took place on December 12, 1894. The examining physicians found that their patient had an irregular heartbeat and was not only disabled by way of his previously stated maladies but also because of "a shattered nervous system caused by same." At the bottom of the typewritten report, the following handwritten note was added: "Claimant has not been able to perform any manual labor for a number of years. Hands do not show any trace of toil." The outcome of this examination is unknown, but a letter Himan sent to the Pension Office in 1912 reveals that he was receiving $13.50 per month. He alleged that since he had turned sixty-six on August 29, the rate should have increased to $15.50.[303] This claim is corroborated by a document noting that he had received $13.50 commencing May 21, 1912, and $15.50 from August 30, 1912.[304]

It is now time to return to Himan's activities in Oswego. Newspaper articles often reported his opinions. In 1898, for example, he criticized President McKinley's message to Congress regarding the Cuban crisis. Said the old veteran: "It was disappointing. It was not as bold as I expected."[305] Himan supported the Board of Education's idea to build a new normal school in Fitzhugh Park.[306] Later that year, many of the local organizations planned to host a military fair, including a bazaar dubbed "The Jungle." The Chamber of Commerce announced it would issue a "newspaper" dedicated to the event, and Himan volunteered to solicit ads for it.[307]

Himan favored street improvements: "In a communication which was received too late to print today, Hiram Dutcher of the East Side strongly favors a street-wide bridge and will give $100 toward the building of such a structure."[308] He also supported causes that honored Civil War veterans: "The City Hall flag was ordered placed at half mast upon the death of any Civil War veteran. Hiram Dutcher was present at the meeting in behalf of this resolution."[309] He also held a strong negative view of increasing tax rates:

> *Hiram Dutcher, referring to the high tax rate, said that all things were climbing. Three years ago, a man got $1.50 on the streets. What does he get now? $3.50. We must look at this thing in the right light. There's two sides to it. This should be done and that should be done...weeds are climbing,*

so are the taxes and salaries. Vote in favor of every special election and you can't expect anything but high taxes. That's what there is to it.[310]

On December 2, 1910, while acting in the capacity of a special policeman, Himan helped prevent the Richardson Theater from destruction when the Oil Well Supply Company's foundry, located behind the theater, caught fire. Prompt action by Himan and Fire Marshal Morrissey prevented any damage to the Richardson.[311] So impressed was Earl Burgess, manager of the Richardson, that he requested that the Common Council formally appoint Himan a special policeman. The motion carried.[312] The year 1910 also saw Himan appointed notary public, a post he was to occupy for a long time. It was perhaps as a result of this position that in 1911, he met wife number four, Rosa Welte. Details about Rosa's life are sketchy, but according to her death certificate, she was born in Germany on July 12, 1866. Their marriage license says her father was Philip Welte and her mother was Catherine Augsburg, both of Germany. Himan had known her only a month when he gave a revelatory interview.

Records indicate that Rosa returned from a trip to Europe aboard the *Southwark*, arriving in the Port of New York on May 5, 1900. She said she was a widow and a cook and gave her age as thirty-two. Under nationality, someone had written "German," but that word was replaced by "citizen." Her final destination was Philadelphia. She said she had lived in that city from 1887 to 1900.[313] The 1900 census shows Rosa Welte, born in 1867, widowed with one child and working as a cook in the home of John Adams in Camden, New Jersey. She said she had come to the United States in 1888 and had lived there twelve years. Ten years later, however, she said she had immigrated to the United States in 1884.

Himan alleged that Rosa had come to Oswego with John D. Higgins and family in 1901, and indeed such a man appears in the local census records and city directories. He was not an import, however, but a native son who in 1899 was the mayor of Oswego and a well-to-do attorney. It is more likely that his wife advertised for a cook and that Rosa applied for the position. It is unknown exactly how long she worked for the Higgins family, but perhaps it was about four years. It is even possible that she lived with them, because not until 1907 does her name appear in a city directory.

In 1905, an event occurred that would alter Rosa's situation forever, and to introduce that, a little background is required. John G. Schneider emigrated from Germany in 1854. By 1870, he was living in Oswego with his wife, Margaret, thirty-four, and daughters Matilda, twelve, and Anna, one.

Between 1870 and 1880, Margaret died. Three years later, John married a woman named Mary who was born in 1840 and immigrated to the United States from Germany in 1861. She died on December 11, 1903.[314] Shortly thereafter, Rosa came into John G. Schneider's life. His daughters alleged that "sometime during the year 1905, said Rose Welte by undue influence induced said Schneider to take her into his household and to exclude all members of his family and all the friends and neighbors whom he had known for many years."[315]

Since Matilda and Anna Schneider are important players in this story, I will digress briefly. Matilda (1858–1945) married Julius Kiehm (1847–1916) in Oswego in 1885 but by 1900 was residing in Chicago.[316] Anna (1869–1930) married August J. Volkman (1862–1916) in Oswego in 1887. Sometime in 1891 or 1892, they migrated to Jackson, Michigan. Therefore, when John Schneider became a widower for the second time in 1903, his daughters were far away and unable to assist him on a daily basis. It would be natural for him to look for a housekeeper. Schneider died on December 4, 1908, and it was revealed that he had deeded his property to Rosa on October 16. The daughters sued Rosa in Supreme Court on December 10, "asking to have a deed and bill of sale of all the real and personal property...given to Mrs. Welte set aside on the ground, primarily, that she exercised undue influence over him."[317] They charged that their father was incompetent and unable to transact such an agreement "although he had never been judicially declared as such."[318] Matilda and Anna further charged that Rosa "induced Schneider to make and deliver to her an alleged bill of sale of all the personal property which Schneider then owned and which was worth many hundreds of dollars; that she induced Schneider to pay over to her money on deposit in banks; that she prevented Schneider from holding any communication with neighbors and relatives as far as possible and so dominated him as to obtain all the property he had had within three years past."[319]

Rosa rebuffed the allegations. She had not prevented his daughters from seeing him and pointed out that they had been in Oswego to visit him during his last illness. She denied that Schneider died intestate, as the daughters claimed. She stated that on or about May 3, he made a will leaving everything to her. She said Schneider left her his estate because she had taken care of him and "supported him during the last summer, when his funds were exhausted." The suit was argued before Justice Rogers in September's Special Term. Mrs. John Lennox, a neighbor, testified on September 28 that Schneider had been in good health until the summer of 1908. She also said he told her Rosa was going to marry him. Some neighbors thought the couple was already married when she moved into his house, and they "gave them a big charivari."[320] Mrs. Lennox further stated, "Mrs. Welte went out working much of the time, being away for several weeks at a time."[321] Despite testimony such as hers, on January 10, 1910, Justice Rogers dismissed the suit.[322] When the census was taken later that year, Rosa (enumerated as Rose Welthey) was living in her new home. She claimed she had no occupation or profession, hinting that not all of Mr. Schneider's wealth had been squandered.

Therefore, When Rosa walked into Himan's office in March 1911, she might not have known him, but he definitely knew her. A jubilant Himan remarked: "It was just a month ago today that Mrs. Welte came into my office and I met her for the first time. I've seen a lot of them in my time, but she just satisfied me, and it wasn't but a fortnight before we had things fixed up. Mrs. Welte is a mighty fine German woman [and] has a cosy [*sic*] little home where I'm sure we will be mighty happy."[323]

Although the bridegroom insisted the engagement was a secret, he and the bride "spilled the beans" when they appeared at city hall to obtain a license. Wrote one reporter: "Mr. Dutcher, confessing to 65 years of age, is as spry as a schoolboy, and to show that he was still in good shape, he did a little dancing stunt in the City Hall this afternoon while obtaining his marriage license."[324] The ceremony took place at the bride's home the evening of April 17. Mabel and Arthur Hart served as witnesses.

Himan settled into wedded bliss for round number four. One cannot help but wonder if his instant attraction for Rosa was the result of her tidy inheritance and "cosy little home." Nevertheless, the two seem to have lived harmoniously until her death in 1919. Himan's regard for her can be seen in the response he gave to a question on one of the Pension Bureau's seemingly interminable forms. When asked if he was living with his wife, Himan boldly wrote, "You bet I am." Life with Himan was probably anything but dull, and Rosa no doubt relished her role as *hausfrau* of a well-known and respected community member.

Himan used his love of fishing to supplement the family treasury, and contemporary newspapers were full of his exploits with fishing gear.[325] In 1914, his skills were really put to the test against a huge sturgeon. Himan was fishing behind the Pontiac Hotel in the Oswego River when his grappling hook "guaranteed to hold a whale" struck something that would not budge. Himan said he had hit a sturgeon, a statement met with derision from his fellow fishermen. The second attempt also struck a seemingly immovable object. The *Oswego Daily Times* reported:

> *Then the fun started. Mr. Dutcher gave a correct imitation of a steam derrick, but nothing came his way. Then the fish got peevish and decided he had already traveled too far up the Oswego River for his health and showed his strict adherence to safety-first principles by turning tail and starting due north. Mr. Dutcher says that he disagreed with the fish, but his objections were overruled, and he started right down toward the lake along with the fish. It was a question as to how long Mr. Dutcher could stay on dry land, but he intended to stay with the fish as long as the tackle held. The argument lasted until the pair were a quarter of a mile from the starting point and near the foot of Cayuga Street. By this time, something of a crowd had gathered to assist Mr. Dutcher. Finally the fish showed his huge head above water for a second and got a wallop just back of it that caused him to lose interest in the proceedings. Mr. Dutcher is one of the liveliest veterans of the Civil War and after his battle with the big fish this morning says he is ready to go to war again any old time. He looks as though he could stand the strain and wear out many a younger man of less experience.*[326]

When measured, the unfortunate fish was over six feet long and weighed 120 pounds.

Himan remained as eager as ever to avail himself of moneymaking opportunities. The 1910 census listed him as a hotel clerk. In 1913, he took a civil service examination for the position of school janitor.[327] In March 1917, he was appointed a notary public with the Pension Department,[328] and he attempted numerous times to qualify for the position of harbormaster.[329] Perhaps his most bizarre escapade involved selling the contents of an antique store owned by "the Kelly boys." According to the article, "Mr. Dutcher met the surviving member of the firm in Virginia recently and got authority to sell out the collection," which was estimated to sell for several thousand dollars.[330] His interest in civic affairs never wavered. He "proclaimed himself ready to go to the front with General Pershing if volunteers are deemed necessary to go to the Mexican border front to protect it from raiders, or if needs be to follow Villa and his band into the mountain fastnesses of old Mexico. While he believes that it is up to younger men of other generations to blaze the trail, still he is willing, he says, to go to the front and shoulder a rifle."[331] The following year, he spoke before a public meeting discussing how to pay for repairs to West Bridge Street. Himan reminded all he had paid for a pavement in front of his home on East Second Street in 1916 "but was willing to do his share toward the damage in West Bridge Street. All citizens should be like he was, Mr. Dutcher said, and this would soon become an ideal city."[332]

Rosa Dutcher, wife number four, was buried in Himan's plot. *Author's collection.*

The old soldier's marriage to Rosa ended on April 25, 1919. She was fifty-two. Her death certificate states that the cause was pulmonary tuberculosis, and an obituary noted that she had been ill for over a year. In addition to Himan, she was survived by siblings Catherine, Teresa and William Welte, all of whom were living in Germany.[333] Himan buried his fourth wife in Riverside Cemetery.

Although an old man, Himan still made deep impressions on people. When asked who was the youngest GAR veteran he had ever met, army recruiter Sergeant Joseph A. Clark replied that it was Himan P. Dutcher, now approaching his seventy-fourth birthday. When told of Sergeant Clark's remark, Himan threw one leg up on a table at police headquarters and replied, "I may not be the youngest, but if there's any younger, I want you to find them. And what's more, I'm going to be just as young at eighty and at ninety."[334] Belying Himan's claims of poor health, the article continued, "Mr. Dutcher reads without glasses, seldom wears an overcoat and can do a jig with less trouble than the ordinary man of his age can climb a flight of stairs."

Himan still had a love for fishing and an eye for the ladies. During the summer of 1920, he traveled several times to Brockville, Ontario, for fishing

Himan Dutcher maintained his good looks well into old age. *Courtesy of the* Palladium Times.

expeditions, making the Revere Hotel his base of operations. There a lady caught his eye. By summer's end, the two had formed a romantic relationship. Her name was Gladys Ruth Griffiths.

Gladys Ruth Griffiths's ancestry is sketchy. She claimed to have been born in England in 1890, an allegation confirmed by her obituary.[335] Her marriage license states that her father was Strudwick Griffiths, born in Canada, and her mother Alice Winton, born in England. The 1891 England census records an Edward Griffiths, twenty-seven; his wife, Alice, twenty-five; and their daughter, Glady [*sic*], five months. They were enumerated in Staffordshire, where Gladys had been born. Ten years later, Edward, Alice and their children—Gladys, ten; Percy, eight; Doris, six; and Norman, two—were residing in Warwickshire. They do not appear in the 1911 census, and it is possible they had immigrated to Canada by that time.

Whatever Gladys's antecedents, Himan found her most amiable. She was the head of the dining staff at the Revere Hotel, and he had ample opportunity to make her acquaintance that summer. Gladys must have acquired similar feelings for him, because by November, they were engaged. Despite rumors swirling through Oswego, "the announcement only came today after the arrival last night of the bride-elect to the city…[she is] a most prepossessing young woman of about thirty."[336] When Gladys came to Oswego, Himan was living in the Arcade Block. After seeing the apartment, she reportedly said, "That's all right for me." The groom-to-be, however, had a surprise: "He suggested they go to call on his sister [Myra]. When they [came] to the house, all the curtains were down. Mr. Dutcher opined his sister was out but said he could get in all right. Entering, he told his bride-to-be this was her house. It is all newly papered and furnished."[337]

Himan and Gladys went to Syracuse to obtain their marriage license on November 10, 1920, and Reverend A.E. Hall married them at the home of Himan's nephew, George Dutcher, and his wife, Constance, who were the witnesses to the union. Both bride and groom lied about their ages.

Himan bought the house at 10 East Fifth Street as a wedding gift for Gladys. *Author's collection.*

Gladys was thirty years old, not forty. Himan said that he was sixty even though he was seventy-four. Perhaps the duo determined that leveling out their ages would call less attention to the marriage. Nevertheless, people noticed. The headline for one article read "Man; 74, Takes Fourth Bride; She's Under 40."[338] Another quoted Himan as saying he was marrying a much younger woman because "he wanted one to outlive him this time." Opined the thoughtless reporter, "It is not only expensive but probably gets monotonous after a while, burying wives. At any rate, that was Veteran Dutcher's explanation when asked how he came to pick such a young wife—he wanted one that would last."[339]

One cannot help but wonder what the bride thought about Himan's crude remarks. In fact, it is difficult to comprehend why Gladys would agree to marry a man who was more than forty years her senior. It was not long before she discovered how much work was involved in caring for an elderly husband. The 1920s were replete with illnesses and applications for pension increases. Gladys's letters requesting advice and financial assistance are heartrending. The troubles began in autumn 1921, when Himan apparently contracted scarlet fever. Gladys mentioned this episode in a letter dated April 18, 1928: "I looked after him when he had scarlet fever, so I guess I can care for him now alright."

However, not all the events in the Dutcher household were unhappy. On January 8, 1923, Himan and Gladys became the parents of a boy, and the old man, proud of his sexual prowess at his advanced age, gleefully accepted congratulations: "Kicking a derby held a foot over his head was no trouble for Hiram P. Dutcher, the youngest 'old Civil War veteran' in this vicinity today. He and Mrs. Dutcher are rejoicing over the arrival of a ten-pound boy. The new son has been named Desmond George Irwin Dutcher."[340]

Himan's feat was announced near and far, and he was dubbed "the oldest father of the youngest child." A very entertaining article was published in the *New Castle News*:

> *The claim of an Oklahoma official to the honor of being the oldest man in the country to become a father is successfully disputed by Hiram Dutcher, 78. The Oklahoma claimant, Frank Vore* [sic], *county commissioner of Muskegon County, is only 70. Dutcher has other claims to notice. He is a veteran of the Civil War who boasts he can walk, run, jump and box with the same zest as when he was a boy of 20. Dutcher has no intention of challenging Jack Dempsey, but he does think he could hold his own at scientific sparring with some of the men who think they can box.*[341]

Himan's achievement was reported as far west as San Francisco, and he received a letter from Civil War veteran Charles H. Blinn on October 24. Blinn, who had been present at the Battle of Cedar Creek, wrote, "I have just read in the dispatches that you are the oldest man in the country to become a father. Aged 78 years, and a veteran of the Civil War. I want to congratulate you, for I believe I am No. 2. I have a daughter aged seven years. Here's to you, old boy, let's try for another."[342]

The state of Himan's health depended on perspective. A short article published on August 29, 1924, congratulated him on his seventy-ninth birthday.[343] Relations with the Pension Bureau, however, were another story. In 1924, he was receiving a pension of fifty dollars a month, an amount he considered insufficient. Documents flew back and forth between Oswego and Washington during the latter part of the year. Himan contacted Thaddeus Sweet, a member of Congress for the Thirty-second District, who in turn wrote to Washington Gardner, commissioner of pensions: "I am enclosing for your consideration the application of Mr. Himan Dutcher, who desires an increase in pension. This veteran lives near my home town and is very feeble. I believe he is justly entitled to this increase and would very much appreciate the early granting of his request."[344]

Gardner responded on October 7:

> *A call has this day been made on the claimant for his sworn statement setting forth as definitely as possible the date from which he first required the regular aid and attendance of another person, and the sworn statement of his attending or family physician, or if that cannot be obtained the sworn statement of his attendant, describing fully his mental and physical condition on the date he alleges that he first required the regular aid and attendance of another person and since, and showing whether from that date he has required such aid and attendance, and, if so, to what extent, and in what particular acts, and that the propriety of having a medical examination made to show the present degree of claimant's disability is being considered, and if warranted, an order for his examination will be promptly issued.*

Himan tried to comply with Gardner's requests. Dr. J.E. Mansfield deposed that "[a]bout Oct 1923, [Dutcher] was afflicted with severe pains across lower back and both limbs. From that date, troubles seemed to aggravate to the extent that constant attention of another party has been necessary. His general physical condition is poor. I believe his condition is permanent and that he will loose [*sic*] entire power of lower extremities." To confirm the doctor's opinion, Gladys also wrote to the Pension Office: "[My husband] is unable to dress or do for himself and needs my constant care. He seems to get weaker instead of stronger, especially if he tries to take exercise."[345]

The Pension Bureau next ordered Himan to appear the fourth Wednesday of each month to Dr. Stockwell's office for a physical. Two days later, on October 17, Gladys wrote frantically to Commissioner Gardner:

> *My husband received a card requesting him to go to Dr. Stockwell's office, but he is unable to go out and walk up the stairs. I phoned Dr. Elder to ask him to come to the house to examine him, but he told me I would have to write to Washington to get a special examiner—so that is why I write. I am anxious if anything can be done, as he seems to get weaker. I have to look after him, help dress and wash him etc. myself. I really need someone to help me.*

The Pension Bureau cancelled the original order and sent a notice to Dr. Elder to conduct exams in a more convenient location. In another exchange between Sweet and Gardner, the congressman, unaware the original order had been cancelled, encouraged Gardner to "expedite the matter" for Himan, whose "health is failing daily."[346] Gardner replied on November 12 that Himan would be examined at home and that his claim would be considered afterward. Dr. Elder performed the examination on November 17. Himan was found deaf in one ear and partially so in the other. His teeth were in bad shape. Worse problems were found in the lower body, including a double inguinal hernia and a very sensitive prostate gland the size of a lemon. His swollen and tender joints had limited motion. Dr. Elder concluded:

> *This man is permanently disabled because of chronic rheumatism and also is suffering from the usual symptoms which accompany an enlarged and inflamed prostate. He requires constant aid and attention of another person because of his inability to get out of bed and wait upon himself. He requires aid in eating and attending to the calls of nature because of the above described disabilities. He is unable to go out of the house even with the assistance of another person. An increase in pension is recommended in this case.*

Himan finally received an increase to seventy-two dollars, retroactive to September 1924.

While Himan maintained that his health was failing, he and Gladys were apparently still having conjugal relations. On March 8, 1925, they became parents of a second son, Lawrence Irving.[347] Naturally, Himan, the "oldest father of the youngest child" in the United States, was eager to share the news with the world: "The proud father of this second child hastened to notify the Palladium of the event and asked that the news be broadcast throughout the land."[348]

Himan's struggle for higher benefits continued into 1926. A letter from Winfield Scott, commissioner of the Bureau of Pensions, informed the old soldier that the Act of July 3, 1926, under which he was requesting an increase from seventy-two dollars to ninety dollars per month, applied only if the veteran was totally helpless or blind. He further stated that documents on file did not demonstrate that Himan qualified. Scott encouraged Himan to obtain a sworn statement from a doctor as to his current physical state.[349] Responding to a lost letter from Gladys, Scott wrote on November 26, 1926, that Himan was not qualified for the increase and further that he had not complied by obtaining a doctor's statement. Gladys subsequently pleaded: "My husband (Himan Dutcher)...asked me to write, as he is unable. He can't do a thing for himself; he seems so weak, as he is 80 years old and has failed terribly lately."[350] It was not until March 9, 1927, however, that a doctor examined him. Dr. Calisch noted, "That the claimant is in bed practically all the time and that he needs constant attendance. That he has arteriosclerosis and organic disease of heart…has attacks of dizziness. That he cannot leave his house; that he has to be attended to in the ordinary duties of his life. At times, he seems mentally deranged…childish…weak. Legs give away when attempting to walk—has to have someone help him walk about the house." The Bureau of Pensions was unmoved. On April 4, 1927, Himan's claim was again rejected.

Himan never convinced the Bureau of Pensions that he was worth ninety dollars per month, although his health steadily declined during 1927 and 1928. Letters written by Gladys to Winfield Scott in April 1928 demonstrate her desperate concern for the old veteran: "For over a week now, I have been washing everyday, as my husband (Himan Dutcher) cannot control himself and cannot walk without my help. Today he went in a dead faint and would have died from shock, the Doctor said. I put cold cloths on his head and got two men to help him on his bed—I thought sure he'd die. I had to leave him with chairs against him while I went to phone for Doctor."[351] Gladys was overwhelmed with the situation. Not only did she have a sick, possibly dying man on her hands, but she also had his half sister, Myra, living upstairs and two little boys who needed food and clothing. She worried about a lack of money: "When I get bills paid, I have no money left, let alone for the Dr. The Doctor said if he is not better to let him know and he would send the ambulance for him to go to Hospital. But unles [*sic*] we could get more money, I cannot let him go, as it's quite an expense over there."[352]

The next extant letter to Scott delivered sad news:

> *My poor, dear Husband, Himan Dutcher, "passed beyond" yesterday at 9 p.m. May 21st. He was not able to help himself since April 14, Saturday, when I had to have the Doctor when he had that shock. If I'd had extra money, I would have had a practical nurse for nights, but I didn't want to run up more bills. I'll be all my life paying them, as I have had to have the Doctor myself. I've got to be well for the sake of our two boys. I am thankful in some ways it is over, as it was so hard to manage all alone, and I know he was glad to be home, altho*[ugh] *he could not say so. Thanking you for your interest. Sorrowfully, Gladys Dutcher.*[353]

Chronic nephtitis was given as the official cause of death.

Himan's stone gives his correct date of birth, which he was not above altering when it suited his purposes. *Courtesy of Darlene Woolson.*

Himan made his final journey on May 24: "Military honors were accorded Hiram P. Dutcher, well-known veteran of the Civil War, whose funeral was held this afternoon at the Church of the Evangelists. Burial was made in the family plot at Riverside Cemetery, where at the grave Taps was sounded and a final volley was fired by a squad from the 28th Infantry at Fort Ontario."[354]

Gladys was now alone with mounting bills, her own health problems and two small children dependent solely on her. She struggled to keep her little family together and to pay outstanding debts. Himan's funeral cost $184, $75 of which had been paid when the Pierce Funeral Home filed an affidavit with the Veterans Bureau on February 27, 1929, to justify a claim for the remainder. So far as is known, the claim was not allowed.

Gladys found herself inundated with concerns associated with single parenthood. She was not entitled to any pension but applied anyway.[355] While initially disallowed, she did eventually receive twenty-one dollars per month for each child. Her own health-related problems caused her no end of stress. Writing to Commissioner Scott, she said:

> *I am so worried, as I am not able to work out just yet, as I have been going to "Health Centre" (as I owe my own Doctor). The Doctor there said I had high blood pressure and to try and rest and not work and have* [a] *milk diet. I already owe $26 for milk, as Himan had to have so much…so I can't have that, as I haven't a cent coming in. I have to get money, as I owe for*

> *funeral, Dr. & drugs etc. Also,* [the boys] *need clothes badly, especially for winter. I am only writing this to explain why I am worried. If you could kindly give me any information on the subject as to what is best to do, I will greatly appreciate it.*[356]

The widow's woes intensified when her lawyer, G.H. Lester, discovered Mary Lodema. The marriage seems to have come to light on October 20, 1928, when the Board of Review issued the following statement: "It appears that soldier had a wife named Lodema Cole, whose death or divorce has not been shown. Soldier says they were divorced November 14, 1865." This was untrue. Lester next received a letter from E.W. Morgan from the Widow Division, asking for information. Morgan, however, misled Lester about the location of the divorce, suggesting it occurred in Oswego County.[357]

Gladys fired off a hysterical letter to Scott: "I am sorry to trouble you, but I feel I must write. I have worried since you wrote Mr. Lester to find out if Himan's first wife was living or dead (he was then 17 or 18 yrs). I heard if not the boys will be illegal children. I know Himan would not have married again if he thought she was living; he was as honest as day in everything and knew the law well."[358] Not until December did Lester verify the divorce:

> *In response to yours of October 30, 1928, and after much effort and search, the decree of divorce…has been located, and a copy of the records, duly certified and under seal of the custodian of the records, is herewith inclosed* [sic]. *I desire to explain relative to the apparent discrepancy in Christian names of plaintiff and defendant. We can only assume that the former had two Christian names, one commonly used and the other only infrequently. And while the correct Christian name of the defendant is Himan, the more common and similar name of Hiram is easily* [substituted] *for the correct one.*[359]

Although Gladys frequently pleaded poverty, she furnished the required bond to become Desmond and Lawrence's official guardian. The hardships she endured, however, are evidenced by a letter sent by Representative Francis Culkin to the director of pensions, evidently in an effort to respond to a plea for help: "For some time, the children of the above named [veteran] have been drawing $42.00 per month. The April check has not as yet come through the guardian, and she is greatly in need of it to supply the children with food and other necessities."[360] Gladys's hardships eventually took their

Although Gladys's stone implies that her middle name was Ann, it was actually Ruth. *Author's collection.*

toll. She died of heart disease on April 10, 1934, and was buried in the Dutcher plot next to Rosa.[361]

Desmond, eleven, and Lawrence, nine, were sent to the Orphans' Asylum on Ellen Street. James A. Kinney, head of the Veterans' Relief Organization, was appointed their guardian by the Surrogate Court on June 14, 1934, and his position was declared in full force on July 12.[362] Kinney (1897–1938), a World War I veteran and businessman in Oswego, was operating a Socony Gas Station. Extensive records document how Kinney accounted for the boys' money to the Pension Bureau. His death in 1938, however, necessitated a new guardian.[363]

Judge Dearborn Hardie (1896–1952) was appointed the boys' guardian on May 26, 1939, and held the position until the case was closed in 1943. He tried to prolong the boys' pensions until they graduated from high school but was refused since the law mandated that payments end when the child turned sixteen.

Desmond enlisted in the U.S. Navy and left Oswego with the Fifteenth Fleet Division in May 1941. He was at Pearl Harbor when the Japanese

The statuette on the Dutcher monument is part of a Smithsonian registry. *Author's collection.*

attacked on December 7, 1941. He served not only in World War II but also in the Korean Conflict and the Vietnam War. Desmond was married twice. His first wife, Molly Fae Hart Benson, was born in 1916 and died in 1985.[364] He next married Philomena Marie Anderson Gessner (born 1923). She died on May 6, 2003, just three weeks before his death.[365]

Like his father, Desmond was active in community affairs. For many years, he was a security officer at SUNY Oswego. He held memberships in the VFW, American Legion, Sons of Union Veterans and Survivors of Pearl Harbor. He was a participant in the unveiling of the naval monument in Oswego's Linear Park.[366] Desmond was a regular donor at Red Cross blood drives. He died on May 27, 2003, and was buried with military honors in Riverside Cemetery.[367]

Lawrence also served in the navy and was honorably discharged in 1945. After graduating from SUNY Oswego, he became an industrial arts teacher. He married Elsie Woodward, from Mexico, New York, in April 1952.[368] Larry, as he was called in later life, eventually moved to Long Island, where he taught in the Jericho School District for thirty years. Upon retirement, he and Elsie moved to New Paltz. Larry died in the Vassar Hospital in Poughkeepsie on January 19, 1997.[369] He had been a member of the Sons of Union Veterans and the New York State Retired Teachers' Association. He was also an amateur radio operator.

Thus ends the story of Himan Dutcher, but not his legacy. Both sons had children through whose veins his blood still flows. His life was long, eventful and, at times, bizarre. Perhaps his greatest achievement was that he never surrendered. That he fabricated or exaggerated his role in various events demonstrates his fierce desire to rise above humble beginnings. "You bet I am!" may truly have been his battle cry. From childhood to his days as a Union soldier to his many wives and, finally, to his lengthy life, Himan Dutcher never yielded to adversity and never permitted his condition to distract him from his goals. Despite his shortcomings, his is a story that deserves to be told.

Notes

Introduction

1. For examples, see *Oswego County Whig*, "Right of Petition," January 25, 1838; *Oswego County Whig*, untitled article, January 27, 1841; and *Daily Times*, "Mr. Polk's Administration," December 26, 1851.
2. Snyder, *Oswego County*, 6.
3. *Brooklyn Daily Eagle*, "Obituary," July 7, 1897, 1.
4. Snyder, *Oswego County*, 6.
5. *Oswego Valley News*, "Oswego County and the Civil War," August 24, 1961.
6. Snyder, *Oswego County*, 1.
7. Phisterer, *New York in the War of the Rebellion.*

Chapter 1

8. *Daily Times*, "Home Sweet Home," July 5, 1851.
9. *Commercial Times*, "Captain Paine's Company of Volunteers," April 30, 1861.
10. Ibid., "Departure of the Volunteers," May 3, 1861, 2.
11. Ibid., "Letter from a Volunteer," May 20, 1861. "S" was probably S.H. Brown. See also *Commercial Times*, "Our Troops at Elmira—Their Condition, Wants, Etc.," May 27, 1861, 2. This article contains a letter from Hamilton Murray, who had visited Elmira and had seen the poor environment in which the men were compelled to live.

12. Proof of Disability, June 25, 1890
13. General Affidavit, June 20, 1890.
14. Deposition H, June 19, 1890.
15. Johnson, *History of Oswego County*, 76.
16. Deposition G, June 12, 1891.
17. *Palladium-Times*, "Oswego Guardsmen Took Part in 10 Battles, Served as Rear Guard on Several Occasions," April 14, 1961, 3.
18. *Commercial Times*, "Letter from a Volunteer," May 20, 1861.
19. Ibid., "Letter from Elmira," June 11, 1861, 2.
20. Ibid., "From the Oswego Volunteers," May 7, 1861, 2.
21. Ibid., "Letter from Elmira," June 11, 1861, 2; see also *Syracuse Daily Journal*, "Excursion to Elmira," June 5, 1861.
22. *Commercial Times*, "Effects of Red Tape," June 10, 1861, 2.
23. Ibid., "The Twenty-Fourth Regiment," June 12, 1861, 2.
24. Ibid., "The Twenty-Fourth," June 24, 1861, 2.
25. Ibid., "The Twenty-Fourth Regiment," August 24, 1861, 2.
26. Johnson, *History of Oswego County*, 76; *Palladium-Times*, "Oswego Guardsmen Took Part in 10 Battles, Served as Rear Guard on Several Occasions," April 14, 1961, 3.
27. *Oswego Daily Times*, "Annual Reunion of the Iron Brigade," September 11, 1903, 4.
28. *Oswego Daily Palladium*, "The Old Iron Brigade," April 23, 1898, 3.
29. Ibid.
30. *Commercial Times*, "The Twenty-Fourth in the Late Battle," September 8, 1862, 1.
31. *Oswego Daily Palladium*, "Campaigning with the 24th," July 25, 1899, 6.
32. Letter written from Poughkeepsie, New York, and dated September 10, 1862.
33. *Commercial Times*, "The Twenty-Fourth Regiment," September 9, 1862, 1.
34. Pensylvania Center for the Book, "Jonathan Letterman," http://pabook.libraries.psu.edu/palitmap/bios/Letterman__Jonathan.html.
35. CivilWar.Bluegrass.Net, "Casualties & Medical Care," http://civilwar.bluegrass.net/CasualtiesAndMedicalCare/ambulancecorps.html.
36. "Medicine and the Battle of Gettysburg," http://members.cox.net/rb2307/content/medicine_and_the_battle_of_getty.htm.
37. Lon K. Savage, "Lee Crushes Burnside at Fredericksburg, VA," *Fair Haven (NY) Register*, December 13, 1962, 6.
38. *Watchman and Democrat*, "Army Correspondence," December 24, 1862.

39. Savage, "Lee Crushes Burnside at Fredericksburg, VA," *Fair Haven (NY) Register*, December 13, 1962, 6.
40. *Evening Star and Times*, "The Morning News," December 1862.
41. Johnson, *History of Oswego County*, 78; see also *Palladium-Times*, "Oswego Guardsmen Took Part in 10 Battles, Served as Rear Guard on Several Occasions," April 14, 1961, 3.
42. *Commercial Times*, "Reception of the Twenty-Fourth Regiment," June 1, 1863, 1.
43. Deposition A, June 6, 1891.
44. *Commercial Times*, October 1, 1863; see also *Oswego Palladium*, "September Local History," October 8, 1891, 4.
45. General Affidavit, May 20, 1890.
46. Deposition D, June 19, 1891.
47. Deposition E, June 13, 1891.
48. Oswego City Directory, 1864.
49. *Commercial Times*, January 11, 1865.
50. For examples, see *Daily Courier (Buffalo, NY)*, "Hancock's New Veteran Corps," December 16, 1864; *Roman Citizen (Rome, NY)*, "A New Veteran Corps," December 16, 1864; *Daily Palladium*, "General Hancock's New Corps," December 28, 1864.
51. *Roman Citizen (Rome, NY)*, "A New Veteran Corps," December 16, 1864
52. *Daily Palladium*, May 8, 1865.
53. The Daily Palladium October 1, 1855, n. p.
54. Ibid.
55. *Philadelphia Inquirer*, "Died," April 10, 1884, 5.
56. *Daily Times*, "Personal," April 23, 1874.
57. *Oswego Daily Times*, "Death of Miss Adriance," May 2, 1874, 1. Her actual death date seems to have been April 30, 1874.
58. Ibid.
59. *New York Tribune*, "City Intelligence," May 7, 1842; see also *Spectator*, "Coroner's Inquests," May 11, 1842, 2.
60. *New York Evening Post*, October 15, 1840.
61. Ray v. Hiller et al., "Reports of Cases Determined in the Supreme Court of the State of Colorado," vol. 11, 445–51.
62. Baskin, *History of the Arkansas Valley*, 517.
63. Clipping located in the Colorado Portrait and Biography Index.
64. Stowe, *Stowe's Clerical Directory*, 190.
65. Hale, *Education in Colorado*, 53.
66. *Decatur Daily Republican*, "List of Letters," July 10, 1879.

67. Corbett and Ballenger's Ninth Annual Denver City Directory, 1881, 71.
68. *Chicago Daily Tribune*, "Deaths," January 15, 1887.
69. The document was signed by E.D. Townsend, assistant adjutant general.
70. Descriptive paged dated February 14, 1927, part of the pension package in the case of Lydia G. Adriance.
71. Letter from Major General Augur, November 28, 1865.
72. Letter to Major R. Chandler, November 29, 1865.
73. Letter to Brigadier General Dent from Major General Augur, November 29, 1865.
74. Letter from Major General Augur dated November 29, 1865.
75. Letter dated December 19, 1865.
76. Deposition B, August 3, 1891.
77. Deposition E, June 13, 1891.
78. Deposition E, August 5, 1891.
79. Deposition D, June 19, 1891.
80. Deposition A, August 3, 1891.
81. Deposition F, August 4, 1891.
82. Deposition D, August 5, 1891.
83. *Millerstown Journal*, April 4, 1885.
84. Deposition 6, August 5, 1891.
85. Deposition A, June 6, 1891.
86. Letter sent from Meadville, Pensylvania, August 15, 1891.
87. Letter sent from Syracuse, New York, June 20, 1891.
88. *Oswego Daily Times*, November 10, 1892.
89. Ibid., "Killed at Oneida," August 29, 1892, 4; see also *Clinton Courier*, August 31, 1892, 1.
90. *Oswego Daily Times*, "Obituary," August 30, 1892.
91. Ibid., "Will be Buried Here," June 28, 1906, 6.

Chapter 2

92. *Oswego Daily Palladium*, "He Fought at Gettysburg," April 11, 1898, 6.
93. *Utica Daily Press*, "Widow of John L. Worden," December 17, 1897.
94. Roberts, *History of Remsen*, 298.
95. Herkimer Archives, "Jefferson Worden"; FindAGrave.com, "Jefferson N. Worden (1838–1904) Memorial."
96. *Oswego Daily Times*, "Letter from Nebraska," August 18, 1893, 3.
97. *Fulton Patriot*, "County Deaths," November 10, 1926.

98. *Post-Standard (Syracuse, NY)*, "Betrothed Girl Is Given Showers," January 26, 1921. See also 1930 census for Salina, New York.
99. Record of Marriages #3758 for Monroe County, New York.
100. *Oswego Daily Palladium*, "To Be Married in Syracuse Tomorrow," January 28, 1921, 7.
101. *Oswego Palladium*, "George F. Pease," June 9, 1933.
102. *Commercial Times*, "Enlist Now and Save Your Bounty," September 2, 1862. See also *Commercial Times*, "The Volunteer Movement," July 11, 1862; *New York Daily Tribune*, "Drafting," August 9, 1862, 4.
103. Phisterer, *New York in the War of the Rebellion*, 3705.
104. *Great Bend Register*, January 18, 1877.
105. *Great Bend Register*, February 8, 1877. For more information on the route taken by the 147th, see Snyder, *Oswego County*, 55.
106. *Oswego Commercial Times*, "From Virginia," October 9, 1862.
107. Johnson, *History of Oswego County*, 84.
108. Snyder, *Oswego County*, 55.
109. Pease summarized in Snyder, *Oswego County*, 55.
110. Pease diary, December 25, 1862, quoted in Snyder, *Oswego County*, 56.
111. The Civil War Archive, *History of the 147th Regiment*, www.civilwararchive.com/Unreghst/unnyin10.htm.
112. *Oswego Commercial Times*, "Letter from Adjutant Farling," 1863. See also *Utica Morning Herald and Daily Gazette*, "The War," January 21, 1863, 3.
113. Commercial Times, "The One Hundred and Forty-Seventh Regiment—The Battle at Chancellorsville," May 22, 1863. See also B.E. Parkhurst, "Letter to the Editor," *Mexico Independent*, April 1902.
114. *History of the 147th Regiment*, 86.
115. Official Report on Chancellorsville Campaign, May 10, 1863.
116. *Oswego Commercial Times*, "The Battle Begun," July 2, 1863.
117. *Oswego Daily Palladium*, "He Fought at Gettysburg," April 11, 1898, 6.
118. Ibid.
119. Ibid.
120. *Oswego Commercial Times*, "From the 147th Regiment," July 28, 1863.
121. Memorandum from Prisoner of War Records.
122. Johnson, *History of Oswego County*, 94.
123. Waterville Times, "War News of the Week," December 3, 1863.
124. Johnson, *History of Oswego County*, 94.
125. *Oswego Commercial Times*, "From the 147th Regiment," December 26, 1863.
126. Ibid.

127. Johnson, *History of Oswego County*, 94.
128. Snyder, *Oswego County*, 65.
129. WebChron, "The Battle of the Wilderness," United States of America Chronology, http://www.thenagain.info/webchron/usa/Wilderness.html.
130. Phisterer, *New York in the War of the Rebellion*, 3705; see also *Oswego Commercial Times*, "From the One Hundred and Forty-Seventh Regiment," May 23, 1864.
131. See an interesting discussion of this problem in Richard Reed, "Lt. Berry Is Presented Sword, Sash by Friends," *Niagara Falls Gazette*, February 14, 1964, 11; see also Roberts, *Andersonville Journey*, 14–16.
132. *Poughkeepsie Daily Eagle*, "N.Y. Conference Veterans at Annual Camp," March 30, 1910.
133. MyCivilWar.com, "Danville Prisoner of War Camp," http://www.mycivilwar.com/pow/va-danville.htm; see also ExploreSouthernHistory.com, "Danville's Civil War Prisons," http://www.exploresouthernhistory.com/danvilleprison.html.
134. "N.Y. Conference Veterans at Annual Camp."
135. "N.Y. Conference Veterans at Annual Camp."
136. Mark Weber, "Civil War Concentration Camps," Institute for Historical Review, http://www.ihr.org/jhr/v02/v02p137_Weber.html.
137. Affidavit, March 26, 1885.
138. Affidavit, March 26, 1885.
139. General Affidavit, March 26, 1885.
140. Letter to John C. Black, November 22, 1885.
141. Affidavit of William H. Rose and Byron C. Earl, July 31, 1882.
142. Affidavit, August 25, 1884.
143. Stibbs as quoted in Genoways and Genoways, eds., *A Perfect Picture of Hell*, 264.
144. Roberts, *Andersonville Journey*, 58–59.
145. Ibid., 59–60.
146. Samuel Eliot, "A Diary of Prison Life: Andersonville and Florence, SC," http://www.pa-roots.com/pacw/reserves/7thres/eliotdiary.html.
147. McElroy, *Andersonville*.
148. Ibid.
149. Ibid.
150. MyCivilWar.com, "Florence Stockade Prisoner of War Camp," http://www.mycivilwar.com/pow/sc-florence.htm.
151. Letter to William Dudley, July 1883.
152. *Commercial Advertiser*, "Reception of the 147th," June 15, 1865.

153. Affidavit, July 30, 1885.
154. Affidavit, August 21, 1883.
155. Letter to William Dudley, July 31, 1883.
156. Affidavit, July 31, 1882.
157. Letter dated July 26, 1883.
158. Letter to William Dudley, July 31, 1883.
159. *Oswego Daily Times*, "Obituary Resolutions," August 26, 1879.
160. *Oswego Times and Express*, "First Assembly District Republican Convention," August 13, 1884.
161. *Oswego Daily Times*, "North Scriba," February 19, 1877.
162. Declaration for Original Invalid Pension, witnessed by Frank's brother-in-law, Joshua Miner, and James Mills.
163. Examining surgeon's certificate, September 14, 1881.
164. Letter to William Dudley, July 31, 1883.
165. Ibid.
166. Affidavit, June 23, 1886.
167. Affidavit of Charles M. Coe, MD, June 12, 1886.
168. *Oswego Daily Times*, "Dressmaking," November 13, 1901, 4.
169. *Palladium-Times*, "Arthur D. Hart, Long in Postal Service, Expires," January 22, 1964, 5; *Palladium-Times*, "Arthur D. Hart," January 25, 1964, 7.
170. *Potsdam Courier-Freeman*, "Duane D. Hart, 73," June 16, 1980.
171. *Watertown Daily Times*, November 21, 1988, 21.
172. *Watertown Daily Times*, March 6, 2005, B4; *Watertown Daily Times*, February 8, 2008, B4.
173. *Oswego Daily Times*, "North Scriba," March 1885; see also *Oswego Daily Times*, May 1885. There is no other evidence that he did indeed travel to New York City.
174. Affidavit, June 12, 1886.

Chapter 3

175. Wildey, *Genealogy of the Descendants of William Cheseborough*, 523.
176. *Oswego Daily Times*, "Mrs. Lydia A. Burnham," May 8, 1912, 8.
177. Regimental descriptive book.
178. Deposition of William Birdsall Miner, May 29, 1918.
179. Bill Young, History of the Eighty-First Regiment, http://www.rootsweb.ancestry.com/nyoswego/military/81sthst.html.
180. *Commercial Times*, "Departure of the Eighty-First," January 20, 1862.

181. *Oswego Daily Times*, "Annual Reunion of the 81st New York Veterans," August 30, 1894, 4.
182. *Commercial Times*, "The Eighty-First—Its Conduct in the Fight," June 10, 1862.
183. Ibid.
184. *Commercial Times*, "The Heroes of the Eighty-First," June 11, 1862. See also *Commercial Times*, "The Eighty-First Regiment," June 16, 1862, which gives a complete list of the dead and wounded.
185. General Affidavit, September 23, 1890.
186. Otis M. Miner, Claimant's Affidavit Before a Clerk, January 29, 1890; William Moore, General Affidavit, January 30, 1901.
187. Claim for Invalid Pension, November 21, 1864. Little is known about Jeffers Boucher. Born circa 1844 in Canada, he enlisted in the 81st on September 19, 1861, and was assigned to Company B. In October 1864, he was promoted to full corporal and on January 1, 1865, to full sergeant. He was mustered out with the regiment on June 10, 1865, at Fort Monroe, Virginia, and promptly disappeared from history.
188. *Oswego Daily Times*, "The Battle of Cold Harbor," June 3, 1910, 4.
189. *Commercial Advertiser*, "From the Eighty-First," July 5, 1864.
190. *Daily Palladium*, "Interesting [Letter] from the 81st," June 20, 1864. The letter was dated June 4.
191. *Oswego Daily Times*, "The Battle of Cold Harbor," June 3, 1910, 4.
192. *Watertown Daily Times*, "Civil War Events of 50 Years Ago Today," June 3, 1914, 4.
193. *New York Tribune*, "June 3, Fifty Years Ago, Grant Made Great Blunder," May 31, 1914, 6.
194. Ibid.
195. See www.civilwarindex.com.
196. *Commercial Times*, "Secesh Letter," October 4, 1864.
197. Town Clerk's Registers of Men Who Served in the Civil War, 1861–1865.
198. Application for Invalid Pension, November 21, 1864.
199. Examining surgeon's certificate.
200. Increase of Invalid Pension, July 12, 1872.
201. Examining surgeon's certificate, March 30, 1878.
202. Declaration for the Increase on an Invalid Pension.
203. *Palladium-Times*, "Election of Officers," December 11, 1893, 6.
204. *Oswego Palladium*, "G.A.R. Election," December 3, 1897, 6.
205. *Richfield Springs Mercury*, "Mrs. Abbie L. Marvin," June 3, 1925, 4.
206. *Oswego Daily Times*, "Lycoming," June 14, 1893, 7.

207. *Palladium*, October 21, 1881.
208. *Oswego Daily Times*, "Lycoming," March 24, 1896.
209. *Palladium*, "An Alleged Assault," September 30, 1880.
210. *Oswego Daily Palladium*, May 19, 1898, 3. Edwin's name is erroneously given as Edward.
211. *Oswego Daily Times*, "Scriba," November 7, 1891, 7.
212. *Oswego Daily Times*, "Enoch Miner," May 6, 1924, 2.
213. *Oswego Palladium*, "Mrs. Alfred C. Lord," March 29, 1888, 1.
214. *Oswego Daily Palladium*, "Rev. A.C. Lord," November 6, 1895, 6.
215. *Oswego Daily Times*, "Lycoming," February 11, 1898; see also *Richfield Springs Mercury*, "Ames-Miner," February 24, 1898.
216. Surgeon's certificate, September 26, 1900.
217. *Oswego Daily Times*, "Scriba," June 2, 1903, 2; see also *Oswego Daily Times*, "Stricken with Paralysis," June 1, 1903, 4.
218. For an Increase of Invalid Pension, December 24, 1903.
219. Physician's Affidavit, December 30, 1903.
220. *Oswego Daily Times*, "Otis M. Miner," March 10, 1905, 8; see also *Oswego Daily Times*, "Otis Miner," March 11, 1905, 4.
221. *Oswego Daily Palladium*, "Scriba," March 30, 1905, 3.
222. *Oswego Daily Palladium*, "G.A.R. News," April 27, 1905, 4.

Chapter 4

223. Tod Bryant, Norwalk Historical Society, www.Connecticutsar.org/cgi-bin/mt/mt-tb.cgil/103.
224. Johnson, *History of Oswego County*, 342.
225. Simpson quoted in Parkhurst, "My Branch of the Parkhurst Family."
226. French, *Historical & Statistical Gazetteer of New York State*, 575.
227. Churchill, *Landmarks of Oswego County*, 153–54.
228. Parkhurst Family Journal, 7.
229. *Albany Evening Journal*, "Legal Notice," August 5, 1857, 4.
230. 1880 Federal Census, Town of Scriba.
231. *Oswego Daily Times*, "Mrs. Fred Marvin," October 5, 1908, 7.
232. Wardwell Robinson, "Union Regimental Histories," The Civil War Archive, http://www.civilwararchive.com/Unreghst/unnyin11.htm.
233. *Commercial Times*, "Orders for the Draft," August 23, 1864.
234 Linda Wheeler, "Once-Forgotten Fort Yields Tale of Black Troops' Heroism," *Washington Post*, October 9, 1998.

235. Deposition dated January 24, 1894.
236. *Commercial Advertiser and Times*, "Fourth of July," June 29, 1865.
237. *Syracuse Courier and Union*, July 10, 1865.
238. Ontario, Canada Marriages, 1801–1928.
239. *Oswego Daily Palladium*, September 18, 1924, 5.
240. *Oswego Palladium Times*, March 9, 1944.
241. *Palladium Times*, January 21, 1937, 10.
242. Ibid., December 12, 1957, 5.
243. Physician's Affidavit, April 7, 1891.
244. Letter from Board of Revision, October 14, 1893.
245. Letter dated June 26, 1893.
246. Deposition C, May 29, 1894.
247. Deposition D, May 29, 1894.
248. Deposition E, May 29, 1894.
249. Letter from Bureau of Pensions, January 25, 1924.
250. *Oswego Daily Times*, "Mrs. Fred Marvin," October 5, 1908, 7.
251. Ibid., October 29, 1909, 8.
252. Letter dated September 18, 1923.
253. Letter dated October 4, 1923.
254. Certificate of Medical Examination, December 6, 1923.
255. Signed on March 12, 1924.
256. *Richfield Springs Mercury*, "Mrs. Abbie L. Marvin," June 3, 1926, 4.
257. *Oswego Palladium Times*, "Mrs. Abbie Lord Miner Marvin," May 25, 1925.

Chapter 5

258. Army Register of Enlistments, 1835–1839.
259. An anonymous contributor to FamilySearch.com offers a marriage date of January 5, 1841, but this allegation has not been confirmed.
260. U.S. Army Register of Enlistments, 1840–1846.
261. U.S. Army Register, 1840–1846.
262. *Oswego Daily Palladium*, "The Youngest G.A.R. Veteran," August 7, 1920, 5.
263. Almira's parents were Albert Coe (1784–circa 1841), born in Southbury, Connecticut, and Phebe Smith (1788–1871), born in Greene County, New York. They married in 1809, moved to Oswego from Herkimer County, where she had been a teacher, and subsequently produced a large family in the town of Scriba. According to the 1865 census, Phebe was

the mother of seven children, six of whom can be identified: Almira, born 1810; Jerome S., born circa 1810; William B., born 1816; Nancy M., born 1818; Hiram B., born 1822; and Mary E., born 1826.

264. In addition to Almira (usually called Myra), the Hortons were the parents of Alvin (1853–1855), Leonora or Nora (1857–1899) and Celia (1861–1863). See Lawson, *History of Union*, 368.

265. *Oswego Daily Palladium*, "Ready to Answer Country's Call," March 18, 1916, 5.

266. *Daily Courier (Syracuse, NY)*, August 24, 1857.

267. See, for example, *Evening Journal (Albany, NY)*, "Horrible Tragedy!" August 26, 1857; *Oswego Daily Times*, "Famous Murder Fifty-One Years Ago," August 24, 1907, 4; *Post-Standard (Syracuse, NY)*, "Murder 62 Years Ago Recalled by Discovery of Old Hangman's Rope," August 24, 1919, 1; *Oswego Palladium-Times*, "Oswego County's Only Hanging May Have Been an Injustice," November 20, 1945, 4.

268. *Oswego Palladium*, "Ready to Answer Country's Call," March 18, 1916, 5.

269. *Oswego Daily Times*, "Famous Murder Fifty-One Years Ago,", August 24, 1907, 4.

270. Ibid., "Trial of Dennis Sullivan," February 9, 1858.

271. The Hibbard murder made headlines in many places, and the anniversaries of the trial and the hanging of Dennis Sullivan were religiously observed in the newspapers. See *Palladium*, "The Old County Jail," January 5, 1888; *Palladium*, "Town Topics," December 4, 1897, 4; *Oswego Daily Palladium*, "Sullivan's Sword Bayonet," September 9, 1899, 5; *New York Daily Tribune*, "Brutal Murder Near Oswego," August 26, 1857, 5; *Buffalo Courier*, "Murder at Oswego, Aug. 25," August 29, 1857.

272. Deposition A, February 25, 1888.

273. Robinson, *History of the 184th Regiment*, 13–14.

274. *Oswego Daily Palladium*, "Memories of the War," April 6, 1898, 6.

275. Robinson, *History of the 184th Regiment*, 17.

276. 1890 Veterans Schedule, Oswego, New York.

277. Robinson, *History of the 184th Regiment*, 41–42.

278. Ellen Fairtile, Gilbert's aunt, wrote about his reception: "The reason [claimant] boarded with me was that his stepfather was cross with him." See Deposition F, February 28, 1888.

279. Deposition of July 1874.

280. Deposition filed June 11, 1874.

281. Deposition entered August 5, 1874.

282. Deposition of October 12, 1874.

283. *Olean Evening News*, "Civil War Vet, 78, Held Oldest Papa," October 22, 1923.
284. *Oswego Daily Times Express*, "Mrs. Mary Dutcher," January 17, 1887.
285. Ibid.
286. *Oswego Palladium*, "Digging for Gold," November 27, 1886.
287. *Oswego Daily Times Express*, "Mrs. Mary Dutcher," January 17, 1887.
288. *Oswego Daily Times*, "Mrs. Catherine B. Dutcher," January 23, 1904, 5.
289. Deposition of Joshua Miner, March 26, 1891.
290. *Palladium-Times*, "Fifty Years Ago," November 22, 1940, 6.
291. Boyd's Oswego City Directory.
292. *Oswego Daily Times*, "Dems Form Combine," February 2, 1900, 4.
293. Ibid., "Memorial Day," April 3, 1890.
294. Ibid., "Grand Army Notes," December 6, 1890, 1.
295. Ibid., "G.A.R. Officers Elected," December 2, 1893, 5.
296. *Syracuse Standard*, July 28, 1898, 7.
297. *Oswego Daily Times*, "Deputy Inspectors," December 23, 1899, 4.
298. *Oswego Daily Palladium*, "Catherine B. Dutcher," January 23, 1904, 4.
299. *Oswego Daily Times*, "Mrs. Catherine B. Dutcher," January 23, 1904, 5.
300. Letter dated October 16, 1893.
301. General Affidavit, October 16, 1893.
302. Letter dated April 20, 1894.
303. Letter dated October 11, 1912.
304. Reissue of Act of May 11, 1912, no date. See also *Oswego Daily Times*, "Big Day For G.A.R.," December 16,1899, 4, and *Oswego Palladium*, "Veterans of the G.A.R.," December 16, 1899, 5, for revealing articles on the efforts of the GAR to get promised governmental benefits for Civil War veterans.
305. *Oswego Daily Palladium*, "What They Say," April 12, 1898, 5.
306. Ibid., "What People Say," February 12, 1908, 4.
307. *Oswego Daily Times*, "Persons Who Will Help Jungle," November 21, 1908, 7.
308. *Oswego Palladium*, "Wisely Favors Street-Wide Bridge," July 2, 1909, 1.
309. *Oswego Daily Times*, "Will Legalize Sunday Movies," January 20, 1915, 5.
310. *Oswego Daily Palladium*, "Pidgeon Talks to Civic League," August 6, 1917, 4.
311. *Post-Standard (Syracuse, NY)*, "Fire Near Theatre: Audience in Ignorance," December 3, 1910, 13.
312. *Oswego Daily Times*, "Department of Fire and Police," December 24, 1910, 4.

313. New York Passenger Lists, 1820–1957.
314. *Oswego Daily Times*, "Mrs. John Schneider," December 11, 1903, 4.
315. *Oswego Daily Palladium*, "Mrs. Welte Has the Deed," December 10, 1908, 8.
316. Federal Census for Chicago, Illinois.
317. *Oswego Daily Palladium*, "Mrs. Welte Has the Deed," December 10, 1908, 8.
318. Ibid.
319. Ibid.
320. Ibid.
321. Oswego Daily Times, "Justice Rogers' Special Term," September 28, 1909, 4.
322. *Post-Standard (Syracuse, NY)*, "Volkman Complaint is Dismissed by the Court," January 11, 1910, 11; see also *Oswego Daily Palladium*, "Appeal Dismissed," March 31, 1910, 4.
323. *Oswego Daily Times*, "Hero of Civil War to Wed," April 17, 1911, 10.
324. *Post-Standard (Syracuse, NY)*, "At Age of 65 Years, Married for Third Time," April 19, 1911, 11.
325. See, for example, *Oswego Daily Palladium*, "Hiram Dutcher's Big Bass," June 23, 1911, 5, and *Oswego Daily Palladium*, "Jeff Cram Has Competition," July 27, 1918, 4.
326. *Oswego Daily Times*, "Hiram Dutcher Gets Sturgeon," May 15, 1914, 4.
327. Ibid., November 4, 1913, 4.
328. *Oswego Daily Palladium*, "Hiram Dutcher, Notary Public," March 10, 1917, 3.
329. *Oswego Palladium*, "Looking Backward [to 1909]," February 27, 1925.
330. *Oswego Daily Times*, "Big Sale of Antiques Collected by the Kelly Boys Now On," August 16, 1921, 6; see also *Oswego Daily Palladium*, "Mr. Dutcher's Busy Days," August 17, 1921, 2.
331. *Oswego Daily Palladium*, "Ready to Answer Country's Call," March 18, 1916, 5.
332. Ibid., "Talk Over City Affairs," March 26, 1917, 4.
333. *Oswego Daily Times*, "Mrs. Rose Dutcher," April 25, 4.
334. *Oswego Daily Palladium*, "The Youngest G.A.R. Veteran," August 7, 1920, 5.
335. *Oswego Palladium*, "Mrs. Gladys A. Dutcher," April 11, 1934.
336. *Oswego Daily Palladium*, "Mr. Dutcher's Wedding Day," November 10, 1920, 4.
337. Ibid.

338. *Syracuse Daily Journal*, November 12, 1920.
339. *Post-Standard (Syracuse, NY)*, "Veteran Picks Young Bride as No. 4 Because He Wants One, He Says, That Will Last," November 12, 1920, 6.
340. *Oswego Daily Palladium*, "A New Son Arrived at the Hospital Today to Mr. and Mrs. Hiram Dutcher," January 8, 1923, 10.
341. *Olean Evening News*, "Civil War Vet, 78, Held Oldest Papa," October 22, 1923.
342. *Oswego Daily Palladium*, "One Old Daddy Sends Greeting to Another Old Daddy," October 29, 1923.
343. Ibid., "He Doesn't Look It," August 29, 1924, 5.
344. Letter dated September 24, 1924.
345. Deposition of October 11, 1924.
346. Letter dated November 10, 1924.
347. *Oswego Daily Palladium*, "New Boy Named," March 10, 1925, 5.
348. Ibid., March 9, 1925, 4.
349. Letter dated September 13, 1926.
350. Letter dated January 29, 1927.
351. Letter dated April 14, 1928.
352. Letter dated April 14, 1928.
353. Letter dated May 22, 1928).
354. *Oswego Palladium Times*, "Hiram P. Dutcher," May 24, 1928, 16; see also *Watertown Daily Times*, "Oldest Father of Youngest Child Dies," May 22, 1928, 16.
355. Declaration for Widow's Pension, May 31, 1928.
356. Letter dated June 14, 1928.
357. Letter dated October 30, 1928.
358. Letter dated November 10, 1928.
359. Letter dated December 10, 1928.
360. Letter dated April 29, 1932.
361. *Oswego Palladium*, "Mrs. Gladys A. Dutcher, 44," April 11, 1934, 5.
362. *Oswego Palladium-Times*, "Letters on Dutcher Estate," June 18, 1934, 7.
363. See *Oswego Palladium-Times*, "James A. Kinney," November 29, 1938, 18.
364. *Palladium-Times*, "Molly Fae Dutcher," November 25, 1985, 2.
365. Ibid., "Philomena M. Dutcher," May 7, 2003, 5A; *Post-Standard (Syracuse, NY)*, Obituary, May 7, 2003.
366. Terry Bennett, "Ceremony Draws Record Crowd," *Valley News*, June 4, 1990, 19.
367. *Palladium-Times*, "Desmond G.I. Dutcher," May 29, 2003, 5A.

368. *Oswego Palladium-Times*, "Dutcher-Woodward," April 14, 1952, 5.
369. *Palladium-Times*, "Lawrence Dutcher, Navy Veteran of World War II," February 5, 1997, 5.

Bibliography

Periodicals

Clinton Courier
Commercial Advertiser and Times
Commercial Times
Daily Courier (Buffalo, NY)
Daily Palladium
Daily Times
Evening Star and Times
Fulton Patriot
Great Bend Register
Mexico Independent
New Haven (NY) Register
New York Evening Post
New York Times
New York Tribune
Niagara Falls Gazette
Olean Evening News
Oswego Commercial Times
Oswego Daily Palladium
Oswego Daily Times
Oswego Palladium
Oswego Times and Express

Palladium
Palladium-Times
Post-Standard (Syracuse, NY)
Potsdam Courier-Freeman
Poughkeepsie Daily Eagle
Richfield Springs Mercury
Roman Citizen
Spectator
Syracuse Courier and Union
Syracuse Daily Journal
Utica Daily Press
Utica Morning Herald and Daily Gazette
Watchman and Democrat
Watertown Daily Times
Waterville Times

Books and Other Sources

Ancestry.com. "An Historical Sketch of the Town of Enfield." http://freepages.genealogy.rootsweb.ancestry.com/~nyterry/towns/enfield/enfieldhis.html.

Baskin, O.L. *History of the Arkansas Valley*. Chicago: O.L. Baskin & Co., 1881.

Churchill, John. *Landmarks of Oswego County, New York*. Oswego, NY: D. Mason & Company, 1895.

Colorado Portrait and Biography Index, 1933–2005.

Cook, Joyce Hawthorne. *The Civil War Diary and Letters of Lieutenant Lansing Bristol, 147th New York Volunteers*. Oswego, NY: Mitchell Printing Co., 2004.

Dyer, Frederick H. *A Compendium of the War of the Rebellion*. Cedar Rapids, IA: Torch Press, 1908.

French, J.H. *Historical & Statistical Gazetteer of New York State.* Syracuse: R.P. Smith, 1860.

Genoways, Ted, and Hugh H. Genoways, eds. *A Perfect Picture of Hell: Eyewitness Accounts by Civil War Prisoners from the 12th Iowa*. Iowa City: University of Iowa Press, 2001.

Hale, Horace Morrison. *Education in Colorado: 1861–1885*. N.p.: News Printing Co., 1885.

Johnson, Crisfield. *History of Oswego County, 1789–1877*. Philadelphia: L.H. Everts & Co., 1877.

Lawson, Reverend Harvey M. *The History of Union, Connecticut*. New Haven, CT: Price, Lee and Adkins Inc., 1893.

Linares, Claudia. *The Civil War Pension Law*. Chicago: Center for Population Economics, 2001.

Marquis, Albert Nelson. *Who's Who in New England*. 2nd ed. Chicago: A.N. Marquis & Co., 1916.

Marvin, Sylvester, and Mary Rumsey. *A Portion of the War Record of the Marvin Family, 1775–1921*. Privately printed, 1921.

McElroy, John. *Andersonville: A Story of Rebel Military Prisoners*. Toledo, OH: D.R. Locke, 1879.

Ontario, Canada Marriage Records, 1801–1928.

Parkhurst, Gary J. "My Branch of the Parkhurst Family." Parkhurst Family Journal.

Phisterer, Frederick. *New York in the War of the Rebellion*. 3rd ed. Albany, NY: J.B. Lyon Company, 1912.

Roberts, Edward F. *Andersonville Journey: The Civil War's Greatest Tragedy*. Shippensburg, PA: Burd Street Press, 2000.

Roberts, Millard Fillmore. *History of Remsen, New York*. Privately published, 1914.

Robinson, Wardwell G. *History of the 184th Regiment, New York State Volunteers*. Oswego, NY: R.J. Oliphant, 1895.

Ryerson, Albert Winslow. *The Ryerson Genealogy*. Edited by Alfred L. Homan. Chicago: Privately printed, 1916.

Snyder, Charles McCool. *Oswego County, New York in the Civil War*. Oswego, NY: Oswego County Historical Society, 1962.

Stowe, Andrew David, ed. *Stowe's Clerical Directory of the American Church*. Minneapolis, MN: A.D. Stowe, 1920.

U.S. Army Registry of Enlistments, 1835–39.

U.S. Army Registry of Enlistments, 1840–46.

Wildey, Anna Cheseborough. *Genealogy of the Descendants of William Cheseborough of Boston, Rehoboth, Mass*. New York: T.A. Wright, 1903.

Index

P

R

S

U

W

About the Author

Natalie Joy Woodall was born in Adams, New York. She holds doctorates in classical languages and English literature. She was a teacher, college professor, journalist and scuba instructor before retiring. She is active in the Order of the Eastern Star, serving as her chapter's secretary. Her passions include her cats and genealogical studies. This is her first full-length book.